Mini Masterpieces
Cross-Stitch
Still Life

Ana Gabriela Pico Villalpando

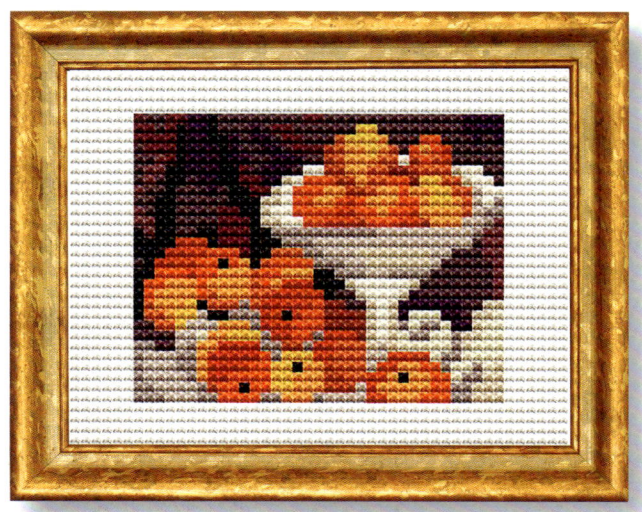

Dover Publications
Garden City, New York

Copyright © 2024 by Ana Gabriela Pico Villalpando
All rights reserved.

Mini Masterpieces Cross-Stitch: Still Life is a new work,
first published by Dover Publications in 2024.

ISBN-13: 978-0-486-85245-4
ISBN-10: 0-486-85245-8

Publisher: Betina Cochran
Acquisitions Editor: Allyson D'Antonio
Managing Editorial Supervisor: Susan Rattiner
Production Editor: Michael Croland
Cover Designer: Peter Donahue
Creative Manager and Interior Designer: Marie Zaczkiewicz
Production: Pam Weston, Tammi McKenna, Ayse Yilmaz

Printed in China by Chang Jiang Printing Media Co., Ltd.
85245801   2024
www.doverpublications.com

Contents

	PAGE
Never Stitched Before?	v
Special Thanks	viii

Pierre Bonnard
The Poppies 2

Gustave Caillebotte
Garden Rose and Blue Forget Me Nots in a Vase 4

Paul Cézanne
Apples and Oranges 6
Curtain, Jug and Fruit Bowl 8
Still Life with Apples 10
Still Life with Apples and a Pot of Primroses 12
Still Life with Skull 14

Paul Gauguin
Still Life with Oranges 16
Still Life with Teapot and Fruit 18

Vincent van Gogh
Irises 20
Majolica Jug with Wildflowers 22
Sunflowers 24
Three Sunflowers 26
Vase of Roses 28
Vase with Carnations 30
Vase with Oleanders and Books 32
Vase with Poppies 34

William Harnett
The Old Violin 36

Shirley Hibberd
Various Ivy Leaves 38

Nora Heysen
Spring Flowers 40

Michiel van Huysum
Branch with a Sunflower 42

	PAGE
Jan van Kessel	
Vanitas Still Life	44
August Macke	
The Ghost in the House Stalls–Still Life with a Cat	46
Little Walter's Toys	48
Édouard Manet	
Moss Roses in a Vase	50
Henri Matisse	
Daisies	52
Geranium	54
Vase of Flowers in Front of the Window	56
Luis Egidio Meléndez	
Still Life with Watermelons and Apples	58
Claude Monet	
Bouquet of Sunflowers	60
Christmas Roses	62
Chrysanthemums	64
Nasturtiums in a Blue Vase	66
Three Pots of Tulips	68
Water Lilies	70

	PAGE
Odilon Redon	
Poppies and Daisies	72
Pierre-Joseph Redouté	
Vase of Flowers	74
Pierre-Auguste Renoir	
Anemones	76
Bouquet of Roses	78
Still Life with Roses	80
Henri Rousseau	
Bouquet of Flowers with an Ivy Branch	82
Still Life	84
H. Lyman Saÿen	
Anemones	86
Robert John Thornton	
Temple of Flora	88
Floris Verster	
Still Life with Zinnias in a Green Jar	90
Black-and-White Charts	92
About Us	104

Never Stitched Before?

READING A CROSS-STITCH CHART

A cross-stitch chart shows you all that you need to know about where to stitch and what color to use. Each colored square (or symbol square) on the chart represents a single cross-stitch. We use DCM color codes in our charts.

TIP: When you begin a new cross-stitch project, start stitching in the middle of the design so that you always have space on all sides. Small arrows at the edges of a cross-stitch chart indicate the center points.

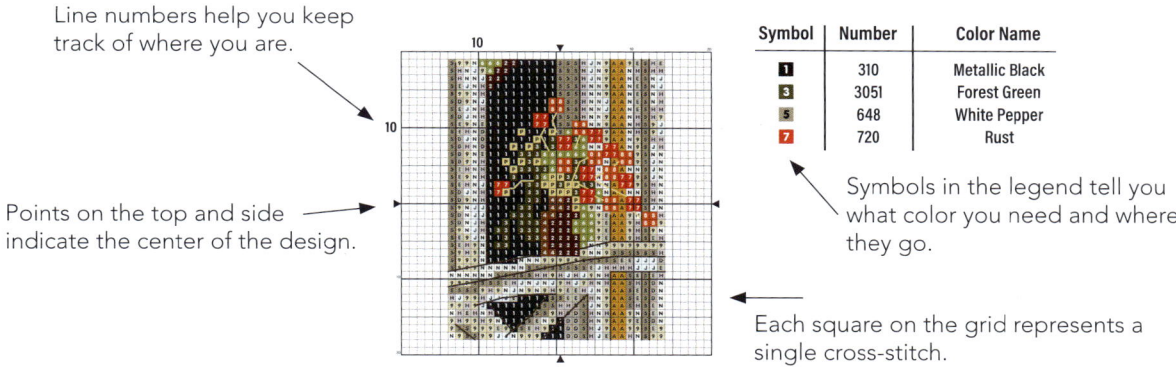

Line numbers help you keep track of where you are.

Points on the top and side indicate the center of the design.

Symbol	Number	Color Name
1	310	Metallic Black
3	3051	Forest Green
5	648	White Pepper
7	720	Rust

Symbols in the legend tell you what color you need and where they go.

Each square on the grid represents a single cross-stitch.

THE FABRIC

Cross-stitch can be done on a number of different fabrics, but the most common is Aida. We use Aida 14, but if you prefer to make smaller versions, you can use Aida 16, 18, or 20. The final measurements can be found in the following table:

	Inches	Centimeters
Aida 14	2.0 x 2.6	5.8 x 6.7
Aida 16	1.7 x 2.3	4.5 x 5.8
Aida 18	1.6 x 2.0	3.9 x 5.2
Aida 20	1.4 x 1.8	3.5 x 4.7

MARK THE CENTER OF YOUR FABRIC

To find the center of your fabric, fold it in half one way and then fold it in half the other way. You can place a pin in the center or make a small stitch.

PREPARE THE HOOP

You can stitch with or without a hoop. If you use a hoop, first loosen the screw and separate the two rings. Place the ring without the screw flat on a table or work surface. Lay the fabric over the hoop, making sure the center of the fabric is in the center of the hoop. Place the other ring over the fabric and press it down. Don't pull the fabric too tight or it will distort the weave of the fabric.

THE FLOSS

We use DCM floss, and the DCM color numbers are included for each project. Most embroidery floss is made up of six strands of thread twisted together. Depending on the fabric you are using, you will stitch with two strands at a time.

THE NEEDLE

A cross-stitch needle has a bigger eye than a sewing needle. The size you use depends on your fabric. Use this guide to help you choose the right needle size.

Aida	Needle Size
14-count	Size 24
16-count	Size 26
18-count	Size 28

START STITCHING

You can stitch each cross individually (from the bottom left corner to the upper right corner) or stitch in rows going from left to right. Starting from the back side of the fabric, bring your needle up through a hole toward the front, leaving about an inch of thread at the back. You will cover the tail with your stitches as you work to secure it.

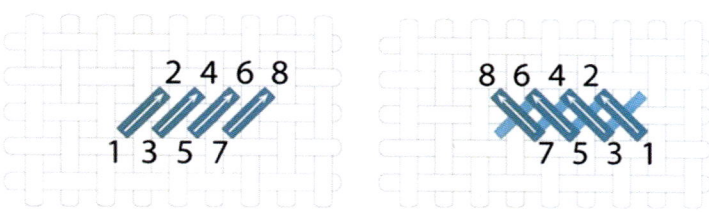

FINISHING

Keep stitching until you reach the end of the thread or until you run out of stitches in your pattern. On the back side of the fabric, pass the needle under at least three completed stitches to secure the thread. Trim the remaining thread.

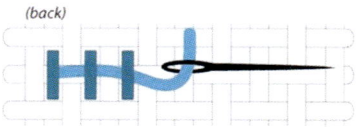

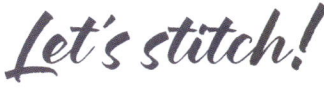

Special Thanks

To our lovely family for believing in us, and for the endless encouragement and support through late nights and long weekends.

To Shannon

(@Crafty_Shananigans),
for your beautiful embroidery and magnificent photos.

Mini Masterpieces
Cross-Stitch
Still Life

Pierre Bonnard

The Poppies

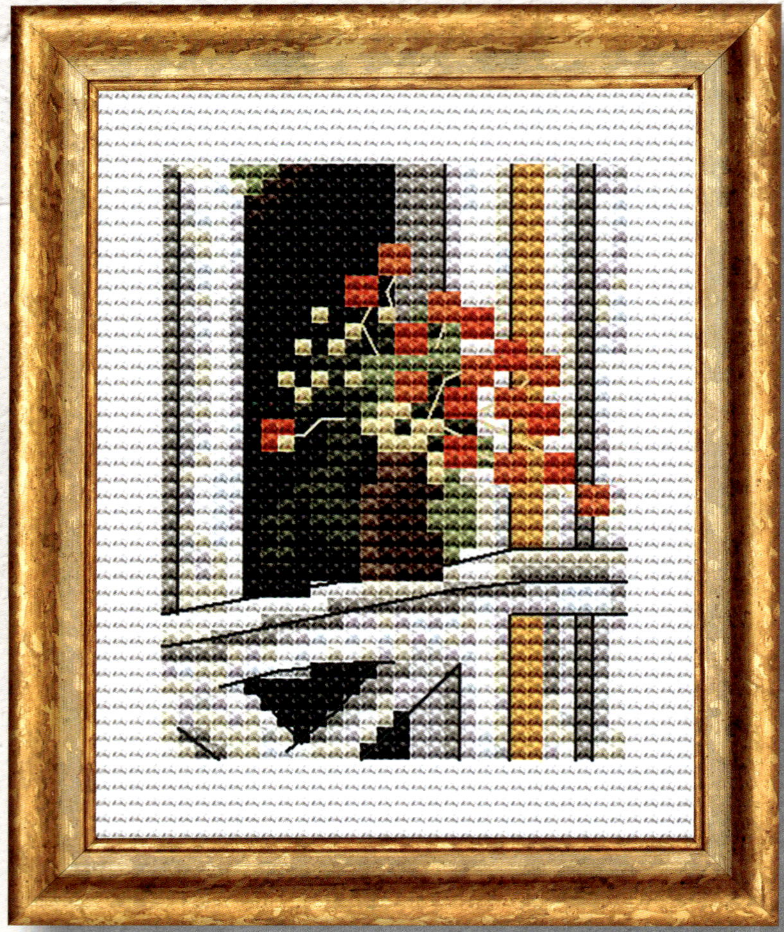

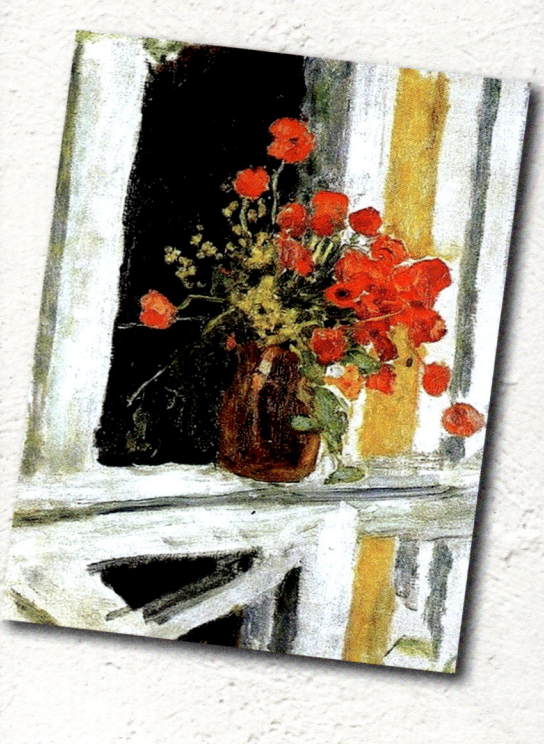

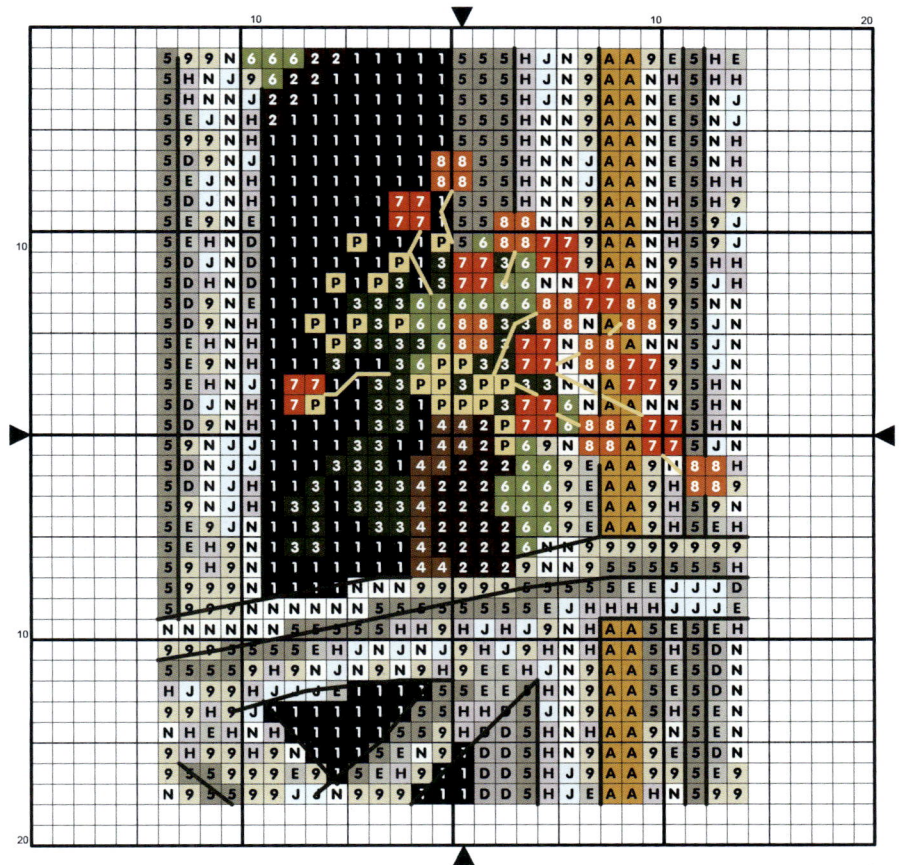

Symbol	Number	Color Name	Symbol	Number	Color Name
1	310	Metallic Black	4	3862	Lama
3	3051	Forest Green	6	3364	Sage
5	648	White Pepper	8	3853	Copper
7	720	Rust	A	3820	Sunshine
9	822	Cotton	E	3072	Thunderous Skies
D	02	Mist	J	3756	Cloud Blue
H	27	Ash White	P	677	Metallic Sand
N	3865	Edelweiss		677	Metallic Sand
2	898	Metallic Ferret		844	Black Pepper

Gustave Caillebotte

Garden Rose and Blue Forget Me Nots in a Vase

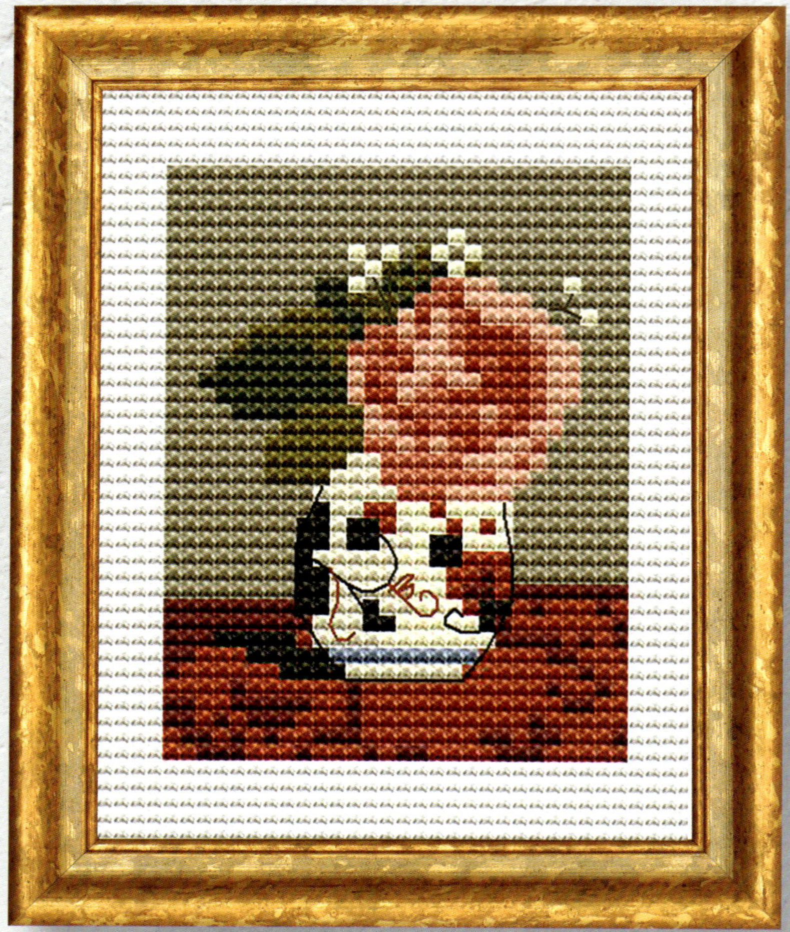

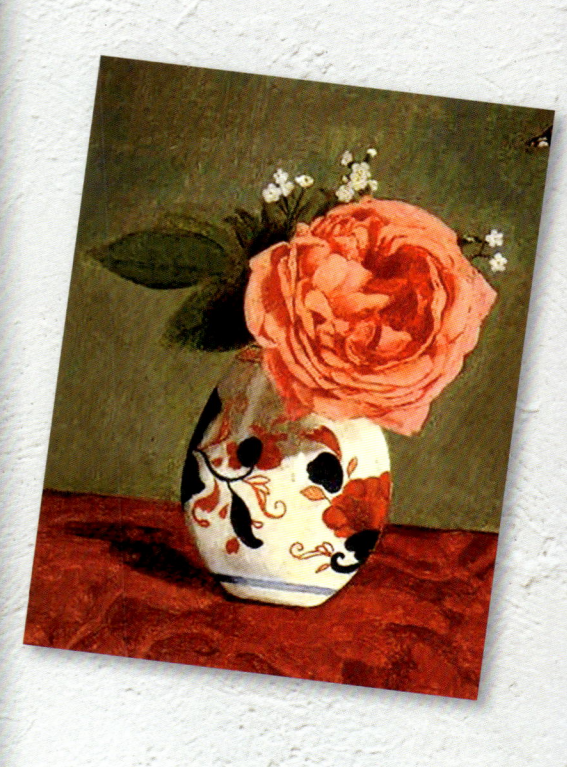

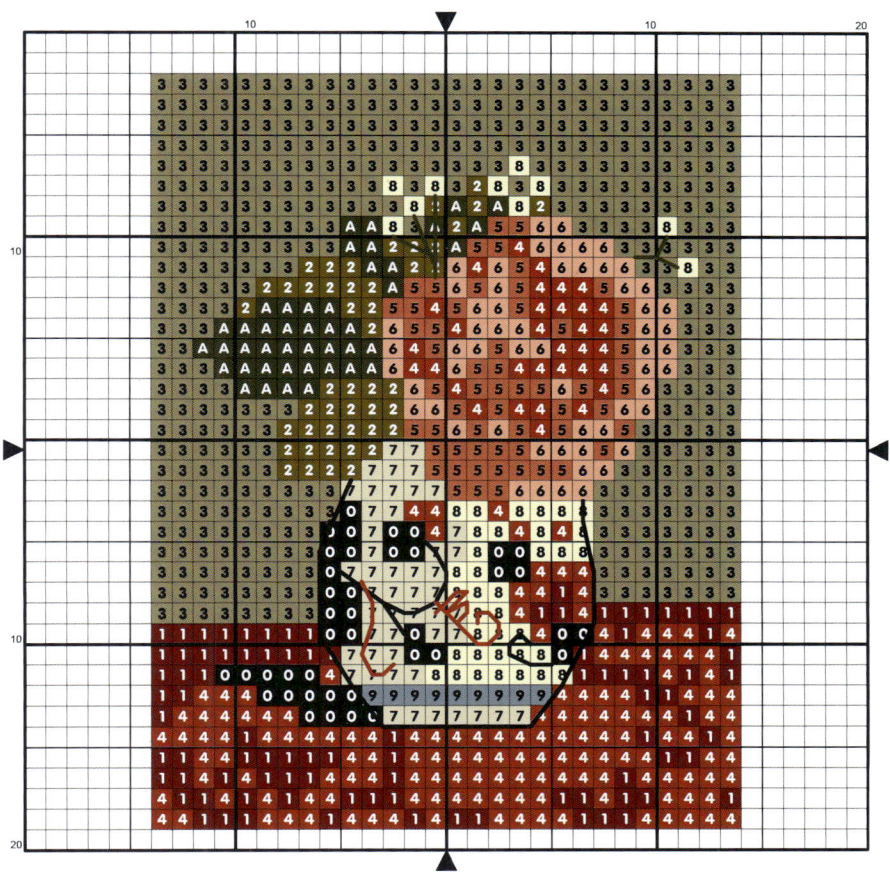

Symbol	Number	Color Name	Symbol	Number	Color Name
0	310	Metallic Black	3	3023	Elephant
2	732	Light Bronzed Green	5	3778	Rose Gold
4	920	Sienna Ochre	7	822	Cotton
6	3779	Burnished Pink	9	932	Blue Gull
8	746	Pearlescent Vanilla	—	310	Metallic Black
A	3362	Conifer	—	920	Sienna Ochre
1	221	Mars Red	—	3362	Conifer

Paul Cézanne

Apples and Oranges

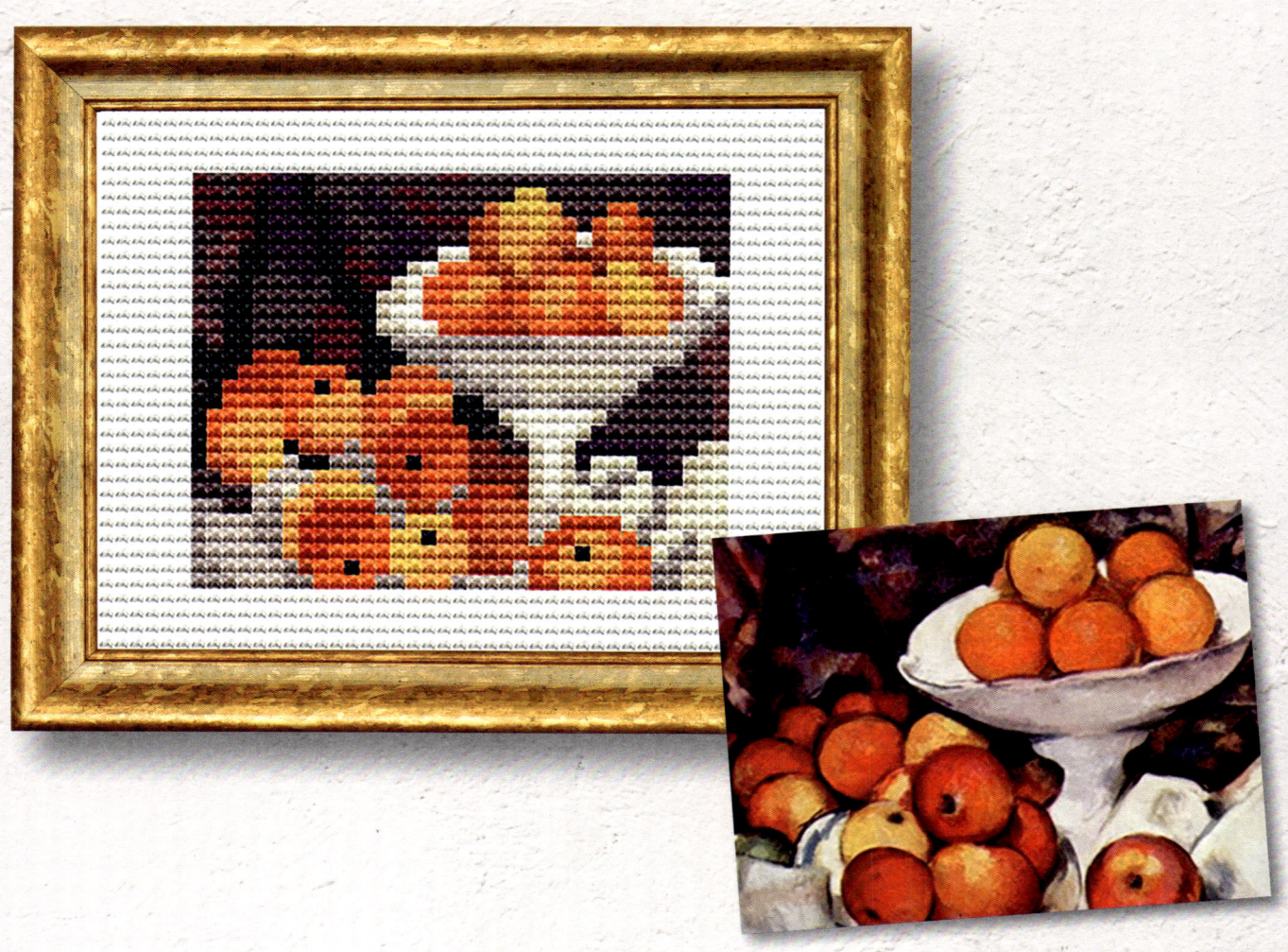

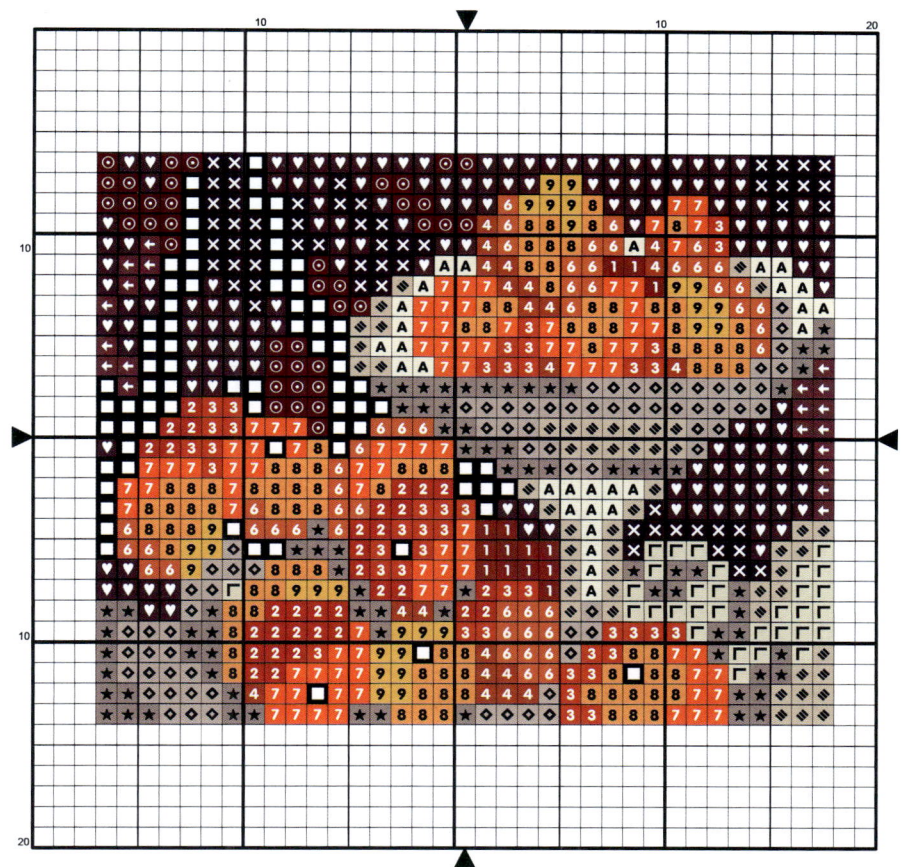

Symbol	Number	Color Name	Symbol	Number	Color Name
☐	939	Elderberry Blue	✖	550	Passionflower
⊙	3685	Metallic Bramble	▼	3740	Gun Metal
←	3726	Iced Plum	1	22	Ruby
2	900	Blood Orange	3	720	Rust
4	921	Tuscan Ochre	6	922	Terracotta
7	721	Papaya	8	3854	Chai Spice
9	728	Mustard	★	452	Pigeon Gray
◆	453	Dove Gray	♥	3033	Ashes
Γ	822	Cotton	A	712	Cream

Paul Cézanne

Curtain, Jug and Fruit Bowl

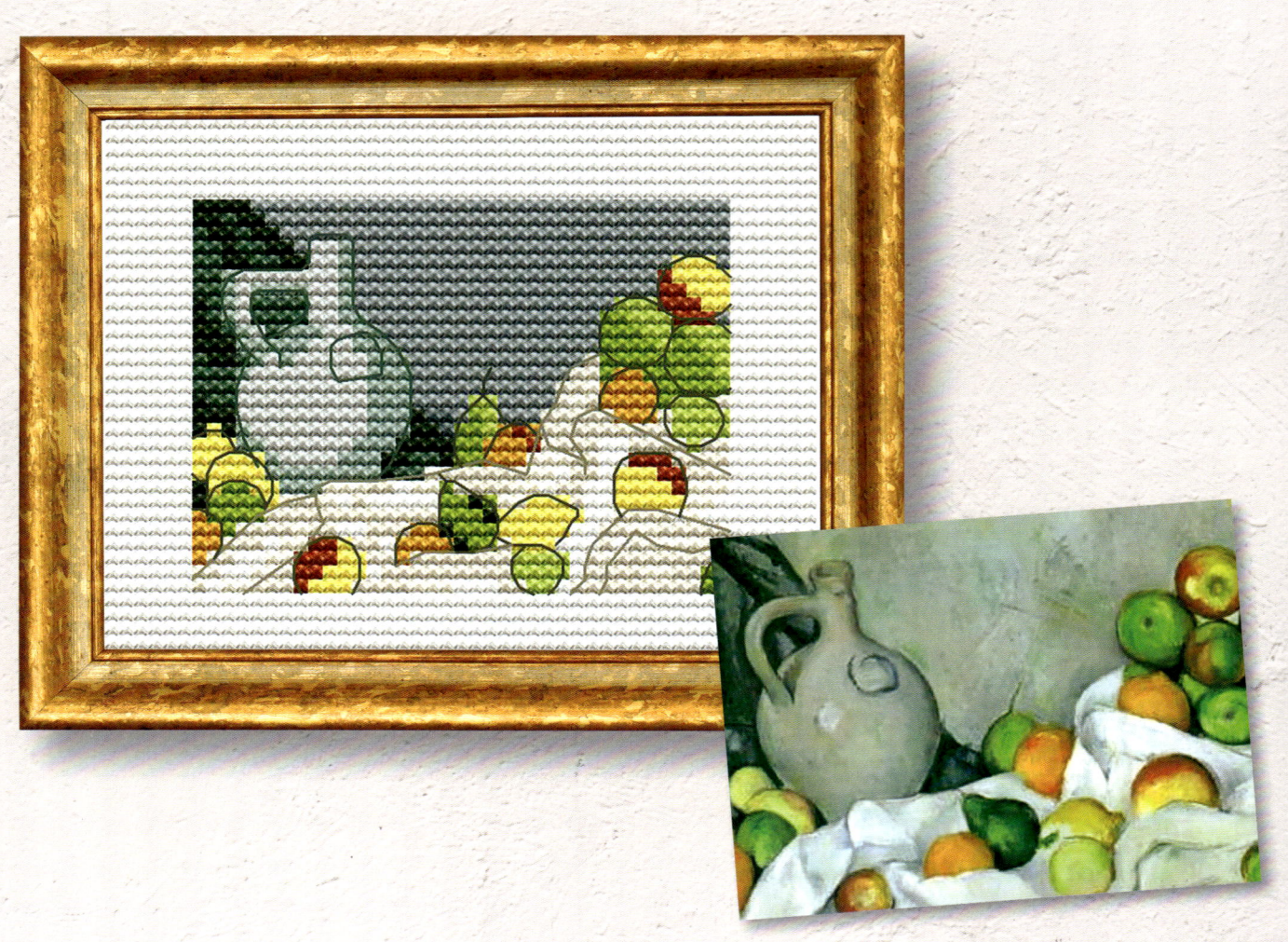

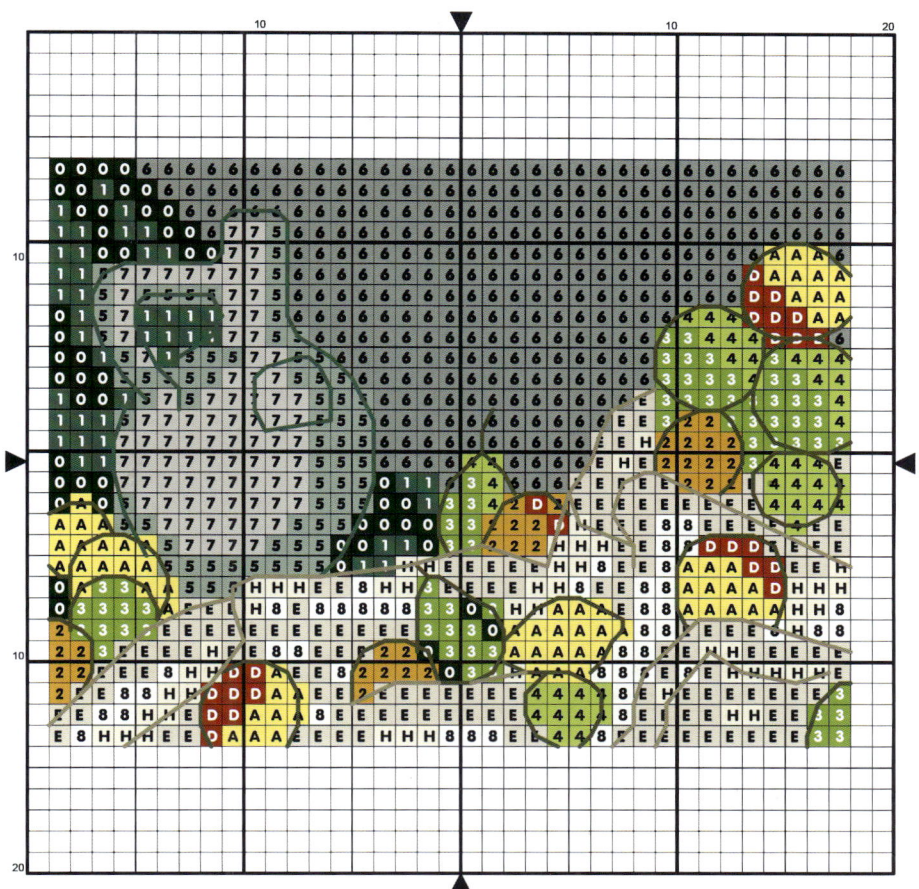

Symbol	Number	Color Name	Symbol	Number	Color Name
0	895	Bottle Green	3	907	Granny Smith
2	3820	Sunshine	5	3813	Lichen Green
4	16	Sprout	7	3072	Thunderous Skies
6	927	Oyster	A	727	Primrose
8	3865	Edelweiss	E	3866	Garlic White
D	920	Sienna Ochre		163	Eucalyptus
H	712	Cream		645	Reindeer Grey
1	163	Eucalyptus		3023	Elephant

Paul Cézanne

Still Life with Apples

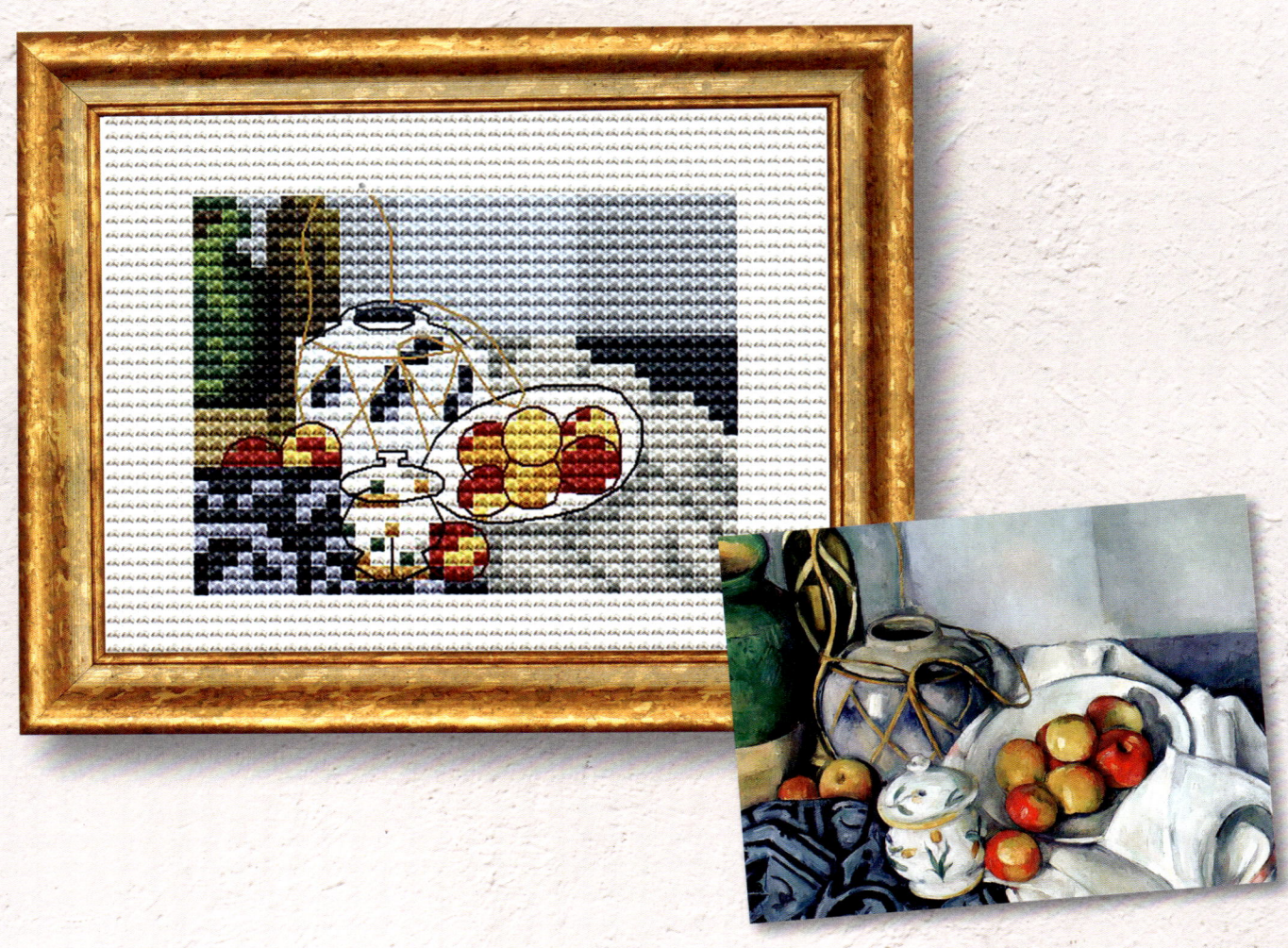

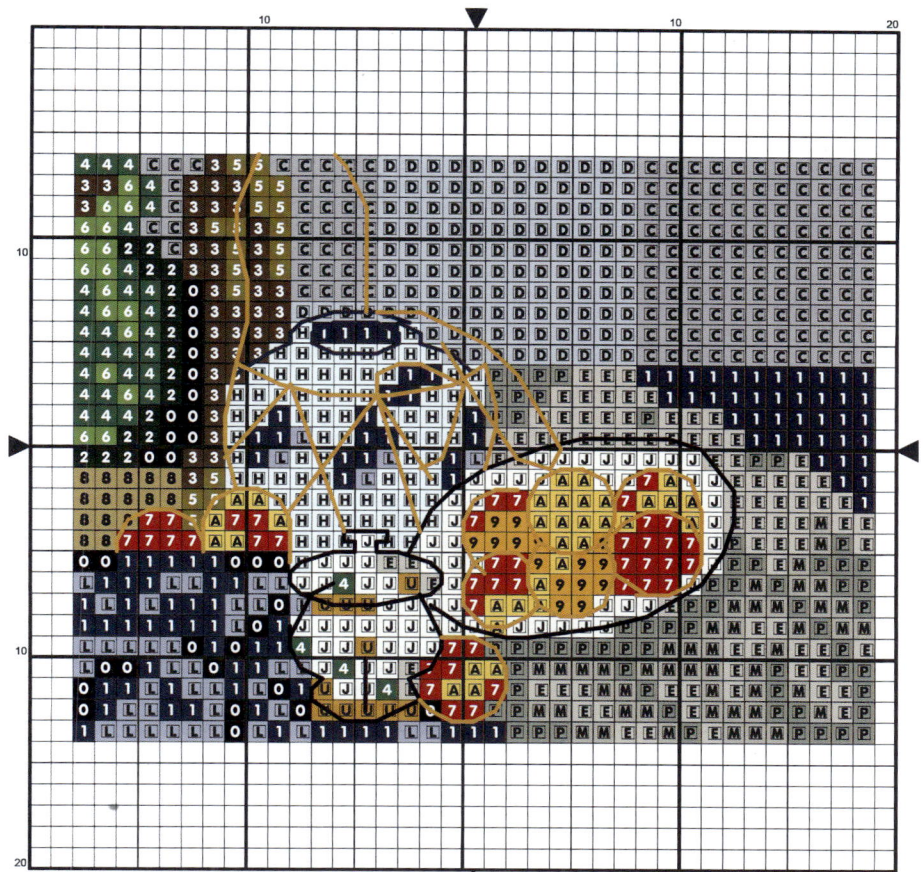

Symbol	Number	Color Name	Symbol	Number	Color Name
O	939	Elderberry Blue	5	3012	Dried Moss
2	500	Ivy	7	347	Egyptian Red
4	3815	Almond Green	9	3820	Sunshine
6	989	Fennel	C	3752	Light Porcelain Blue
8	613	Twine	E	3072	Thunderous Skies
A	3822	Corn Husk	J	3865	Edelweiss
D	3753	Moonlight Blue	M	928	Oyster Shell
H	3756	Cloud Blue	U	729	Honey
L	157	Heliotrope		939	Elderberry Blue
P	927	Oyster		930	Slate Grey
1	930	Slate Grey		729	Honey
3	3787	Grey Wolf		814	Vin Rouge

11

Paul Cézanne

Still Life with Apples and a Pot of Primroses

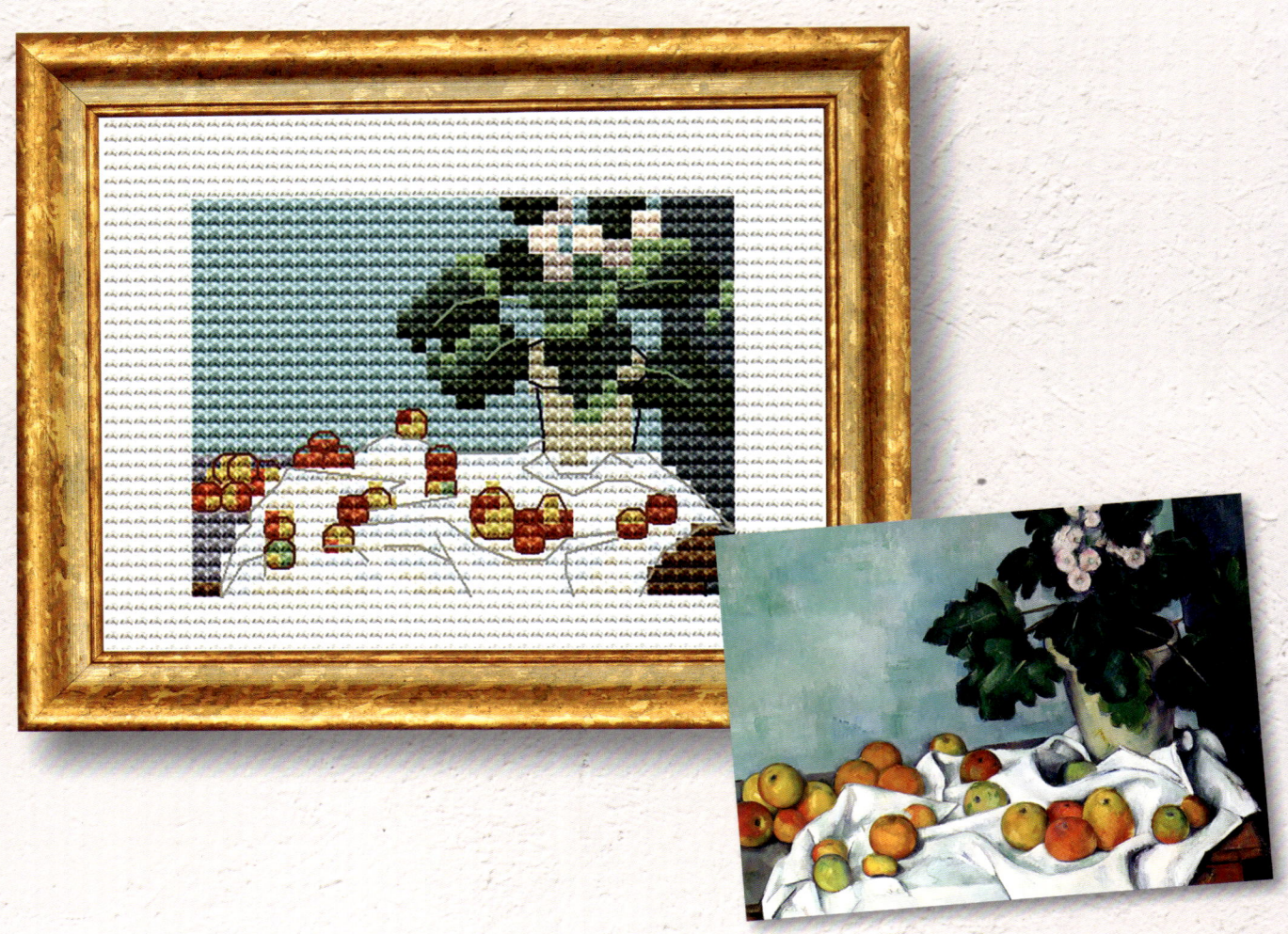

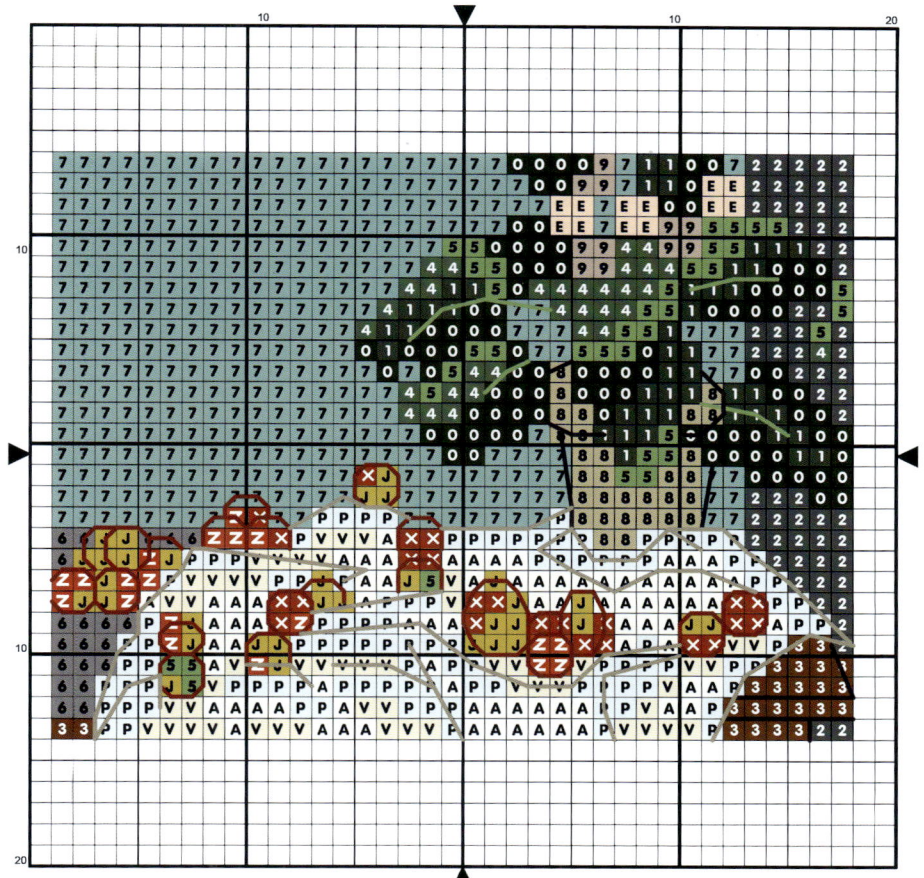

Symbol	Number	Color Name	Symbol	Number	Color Name
O	895	Bottle Green	5	368	Eau de Nile
2	3768	Storm	7	598	Pale Lagoon
4	163	Eucalyptus	9	453	Dove Gray
6	318	Granite Grey	E	948	Himalayan Salt
8	644	Hemp	P	3756	Cloud Blue
A	3865	Edelweiss	Z	921	Tuscan Ochre
J	834	Dusty Sunflower		368	Eau de Nile
V	712	Cream		823	Blueberry
X	920	Sienna Ochre		918	Rosewood
1	501	Pond Green		648	White Pepper
3	869	Coffee			

Paul Cézanne

Still Life with Skull

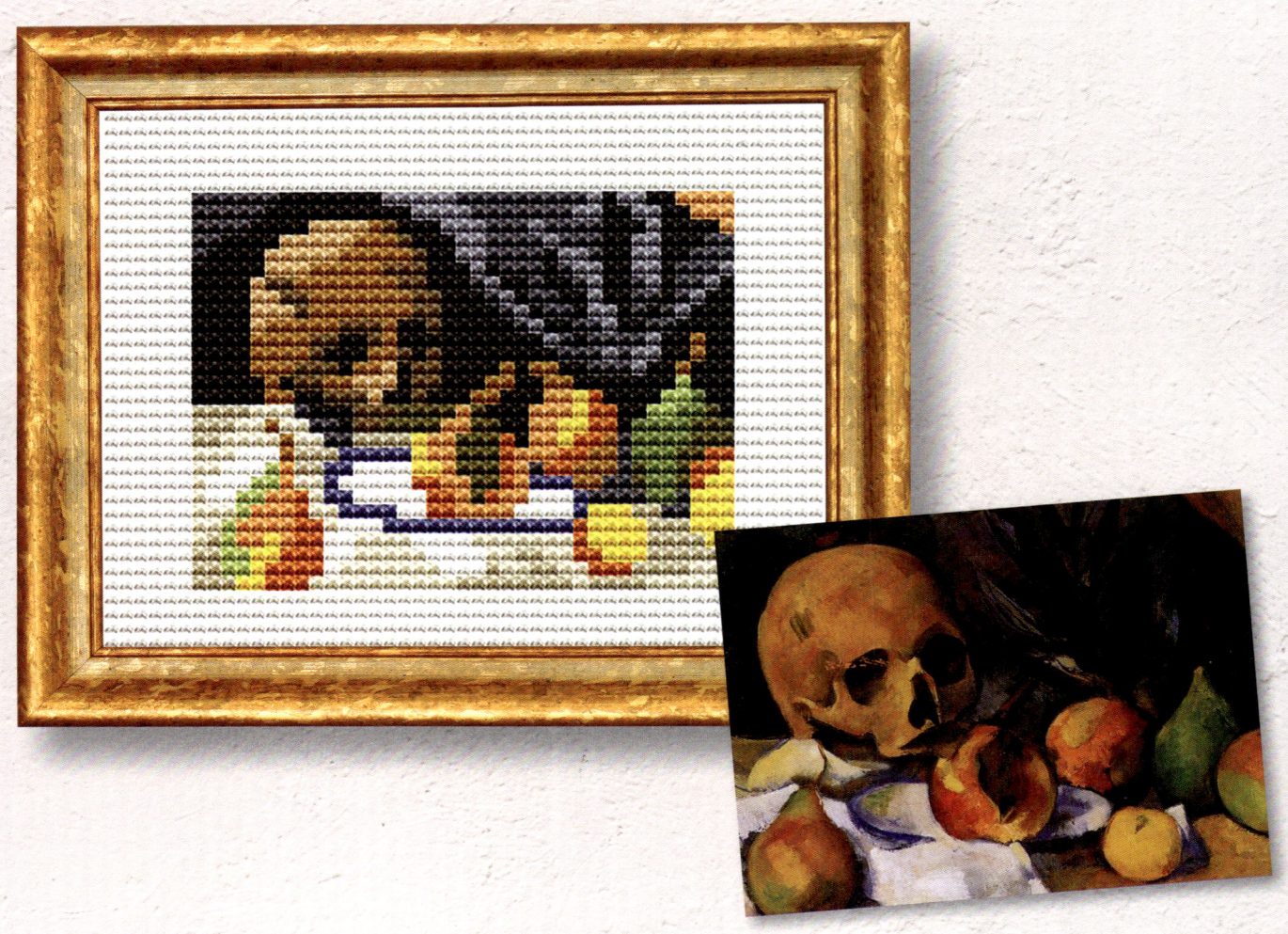

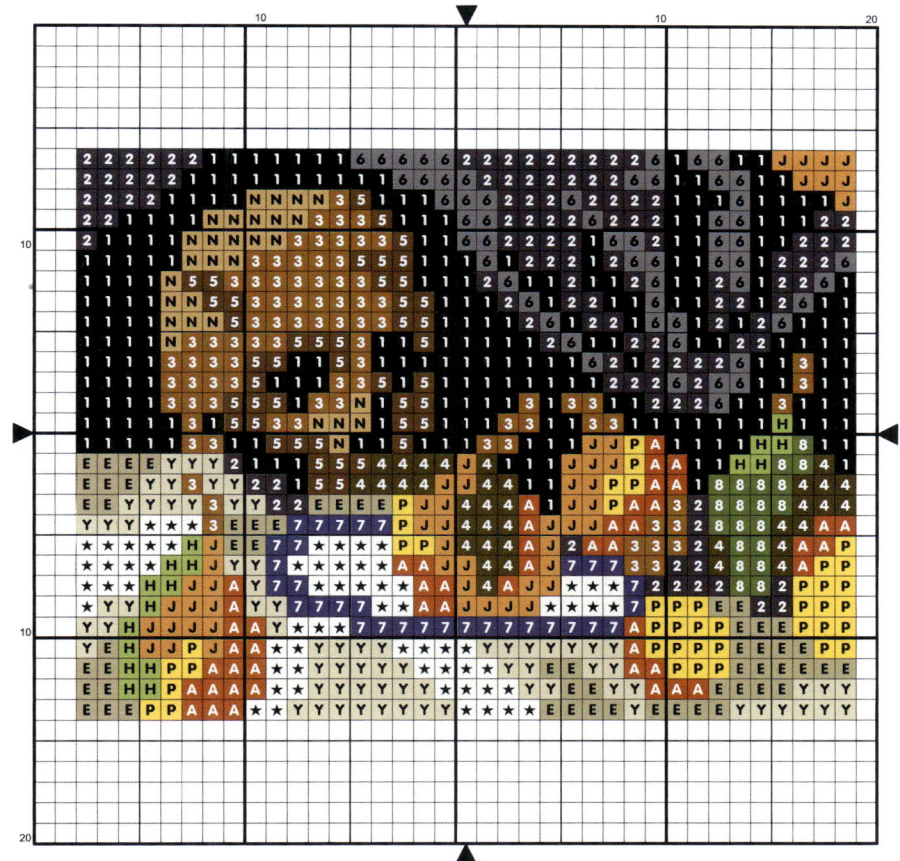

Symbol	Number	Color Name	Symbol	Number	Color Name
1	310	Metallic Black	2	317	Metallic Steel
3	680	Fennec	4	3011	Deep Olive
5	611	Umber	6	318	Granite Grey
7	793	Deep Ocean	8	3347	Asparagus
A	976	Nutmeg	E	644	Hemp
H	3348	Scallion	J	3827	Coral Blush
N	738	Sahara	P	726	Mimosa
Y	822	Cotton	★	3865	Edelweiss

Paul Gauguin

Still Life with Oranges

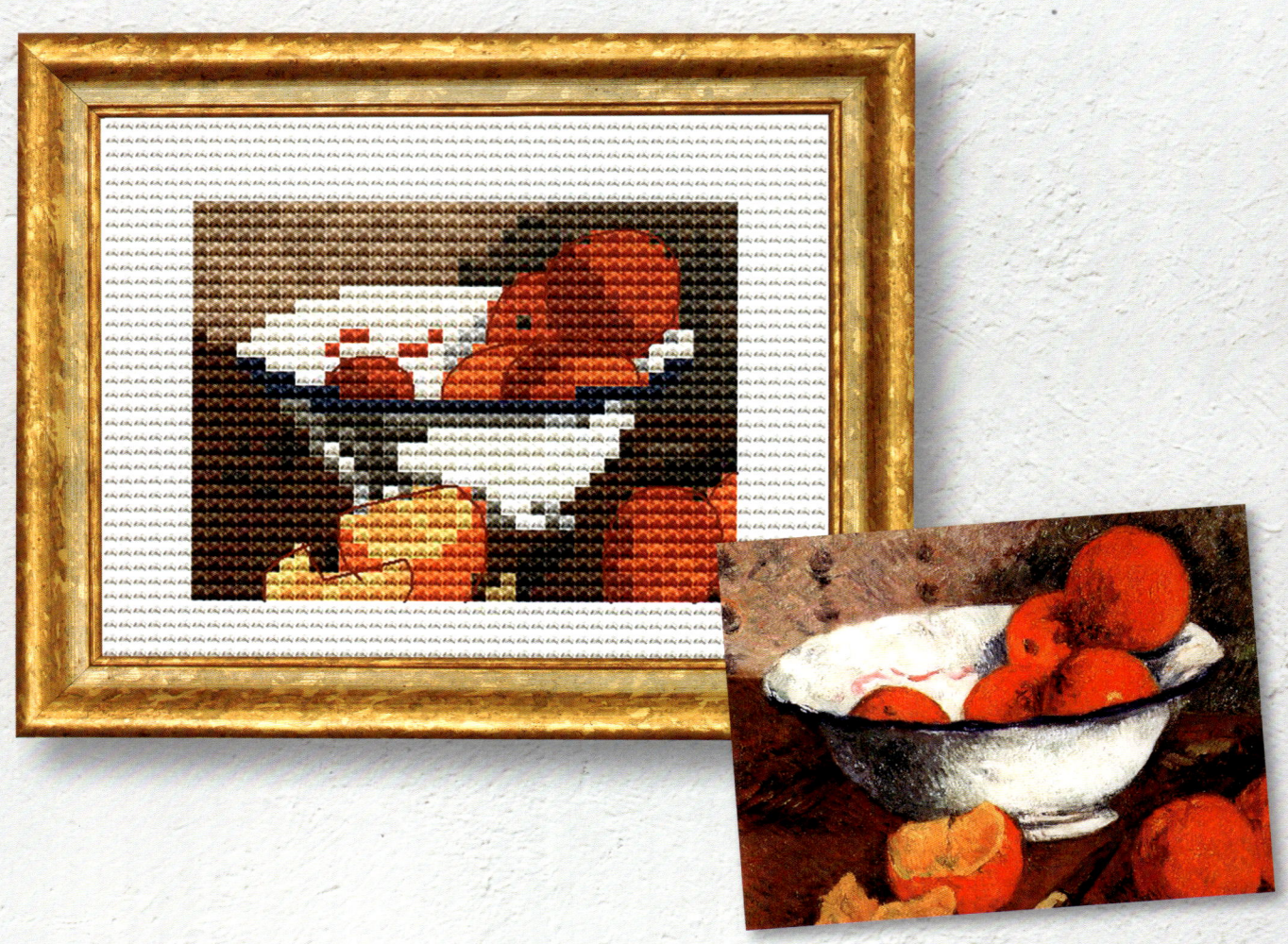

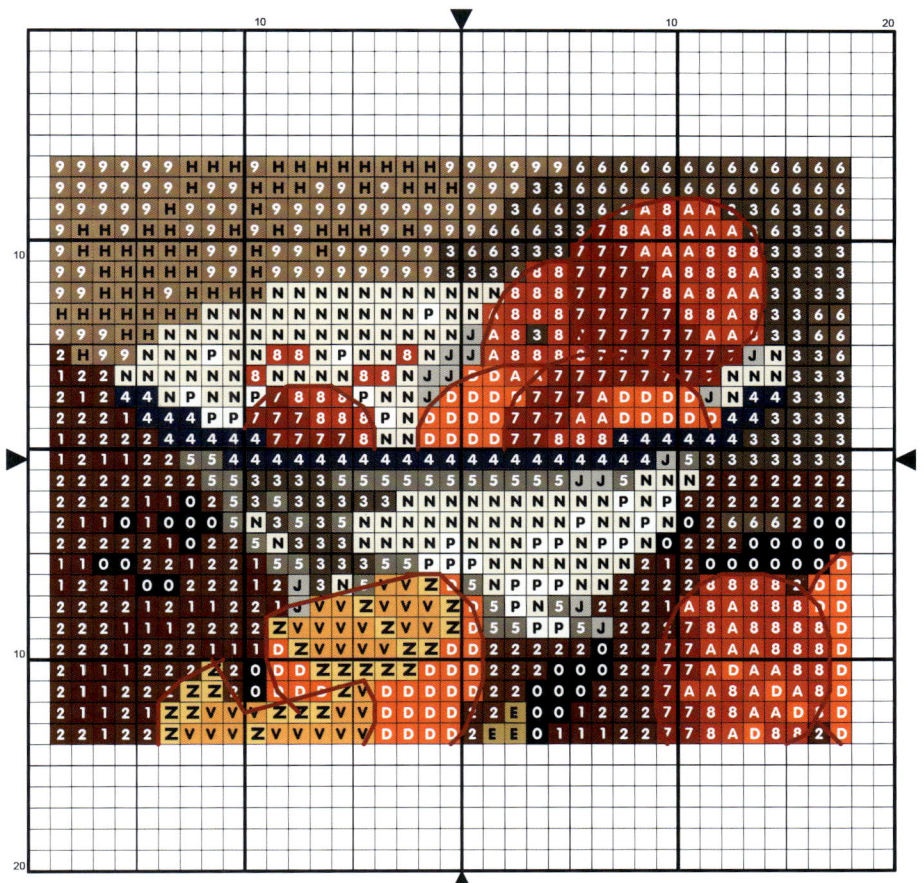

Symbol	Number	Color Name	Symbol	Number	Color Name
0	3371	Peppercorn	1	3857	Oxblood
2	801	Mink	3	3787	Grey Wolf
4	3750	Dark Petrol Blue	5	647	Rock Grey
6	08	Racoon	7	919	Terracotta Brown
8	900	Blood Orange	9	841	Suede
A	720	Rust	D	721	Papaya
E	422	Light Oak	H	3864	Vicuna Wool
J	928	Oyster Shell	N	712	Cream
P	3865	Edelweiss	V	3854	Chai Spice
Z	3855	Desert Winds		919	Terracotta Brown

Paul Gauguin

Still Life with Teapot and Fruit

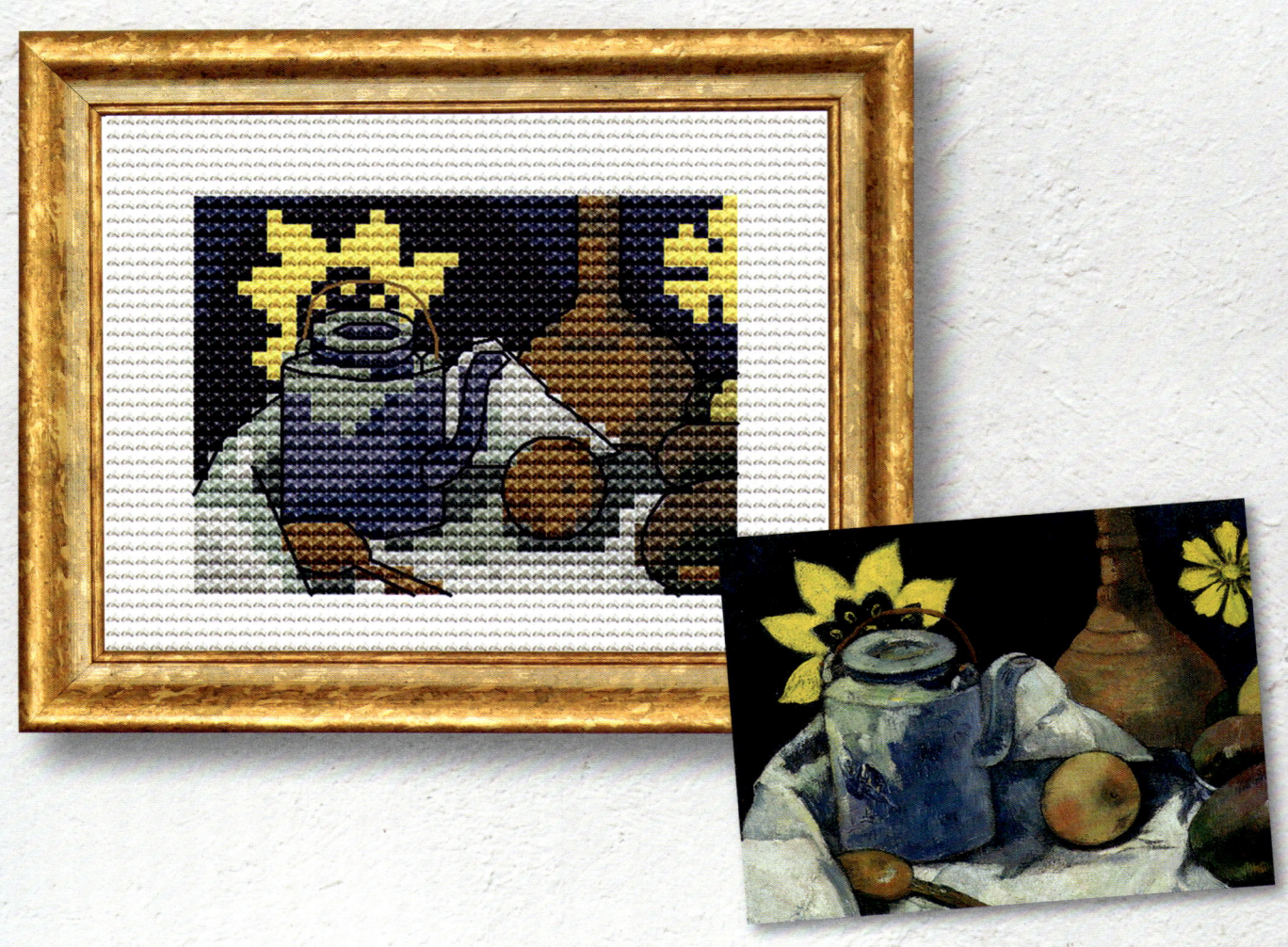

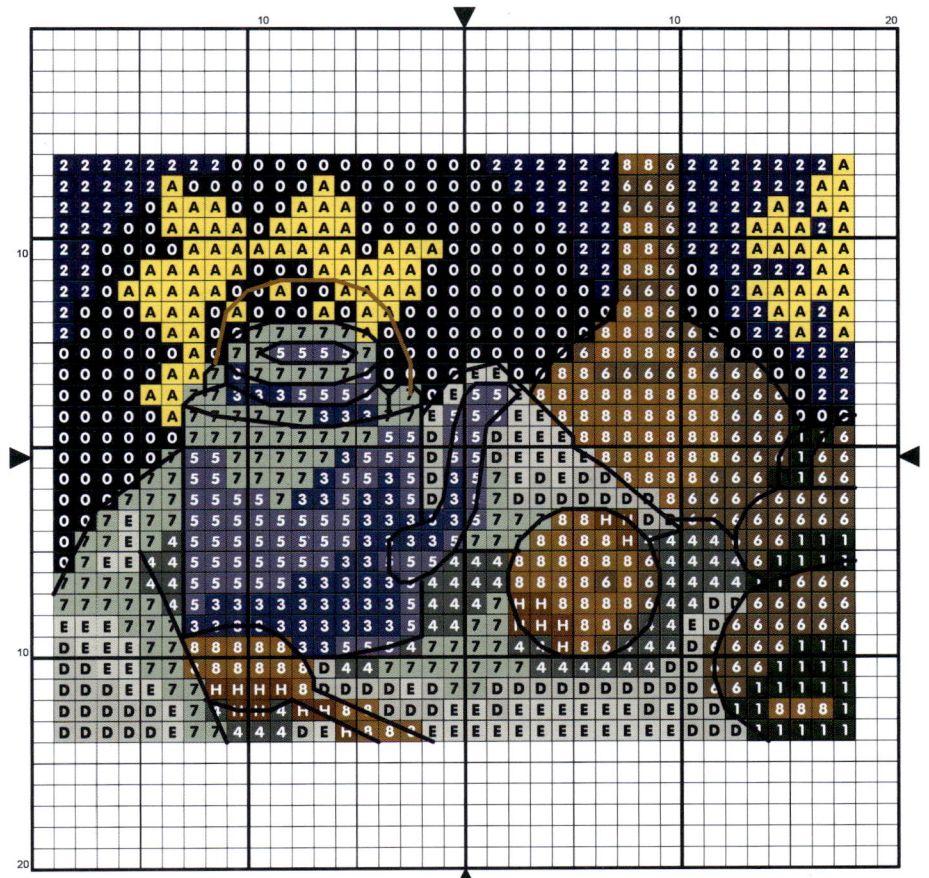

Symbol	Number	Color Name	Symbol	Number	Color Name
0	823	Blueberry	3	312	Midnight Blue
2	803	Inky Blue	5	161	Blue Ash
4	3768	Storm	7	3813	Lichen Green
6	08	Racoon	A	726	Mimosa
8	420	Hazelnut	E	3072	Thunderous Skies
D	928	Oyster Shell	—	823	Blueberry
H	869	Coffee	—	420	Hazelnut
1	500	Ivy			

Vincent van Gogh

Irises

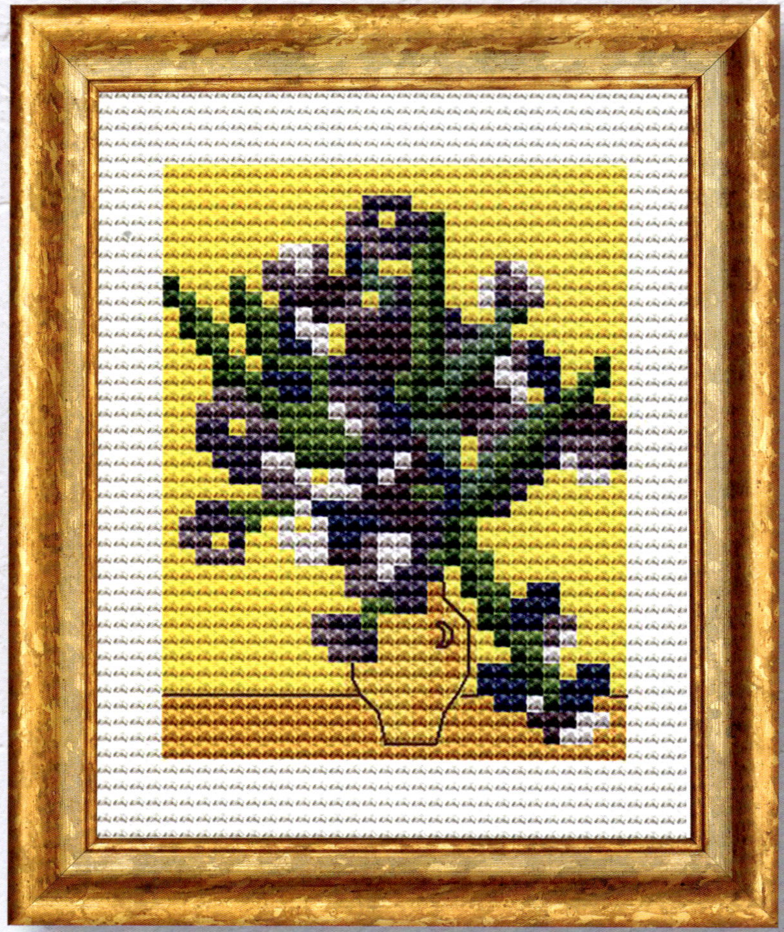

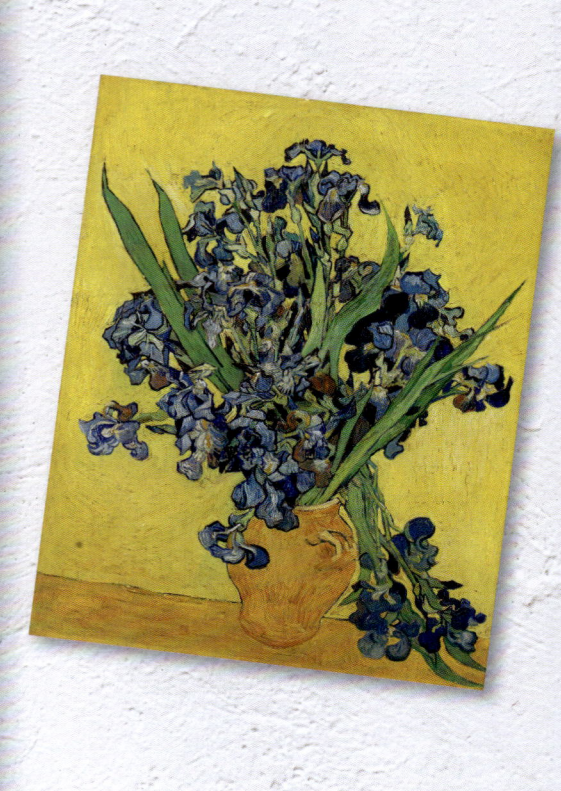

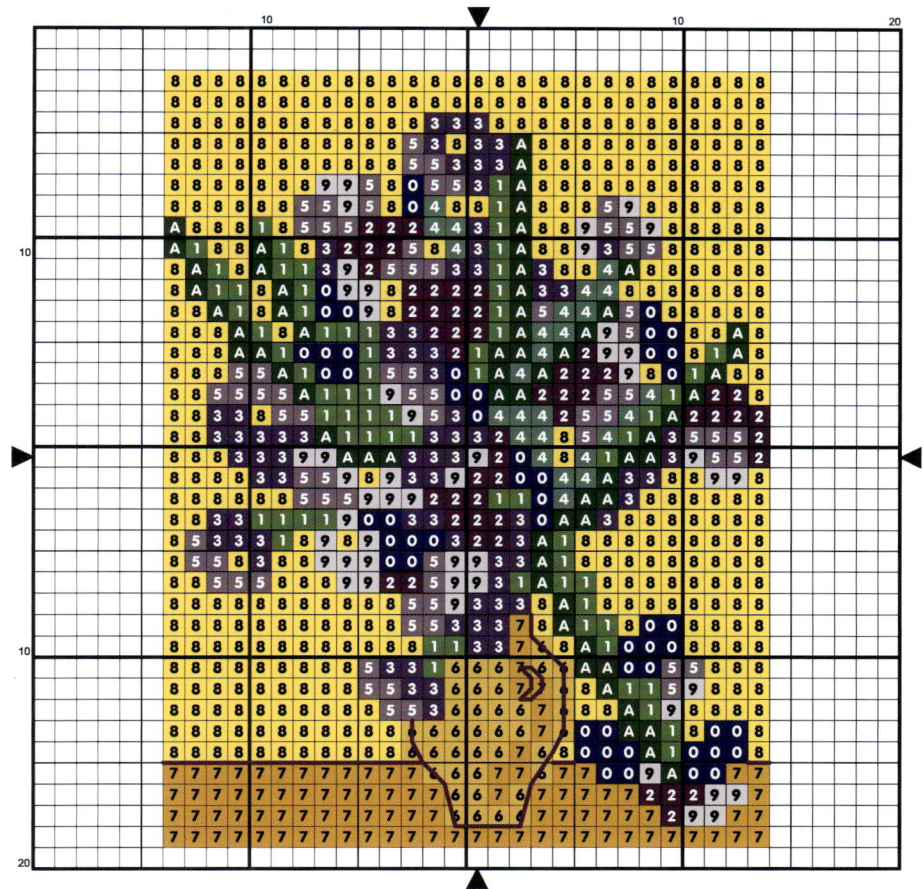

Symbol	Number	Color Name	Symbol	Number	Color Name
O	824	Marine Blue	1	988	Verbena Stem
2	29	Emperor Purple	3	32	Antique Mauve
4	3816	Serpent	5	28	Lavender Gray
6	3821	Metallic Mango	7	3820	Sunshine
8	726	Mimosa	9	27	Ash White
A	986	Boxwood		29	Emperor Purple

Vincent van Gogh

Majolica Jug with Wildflowers

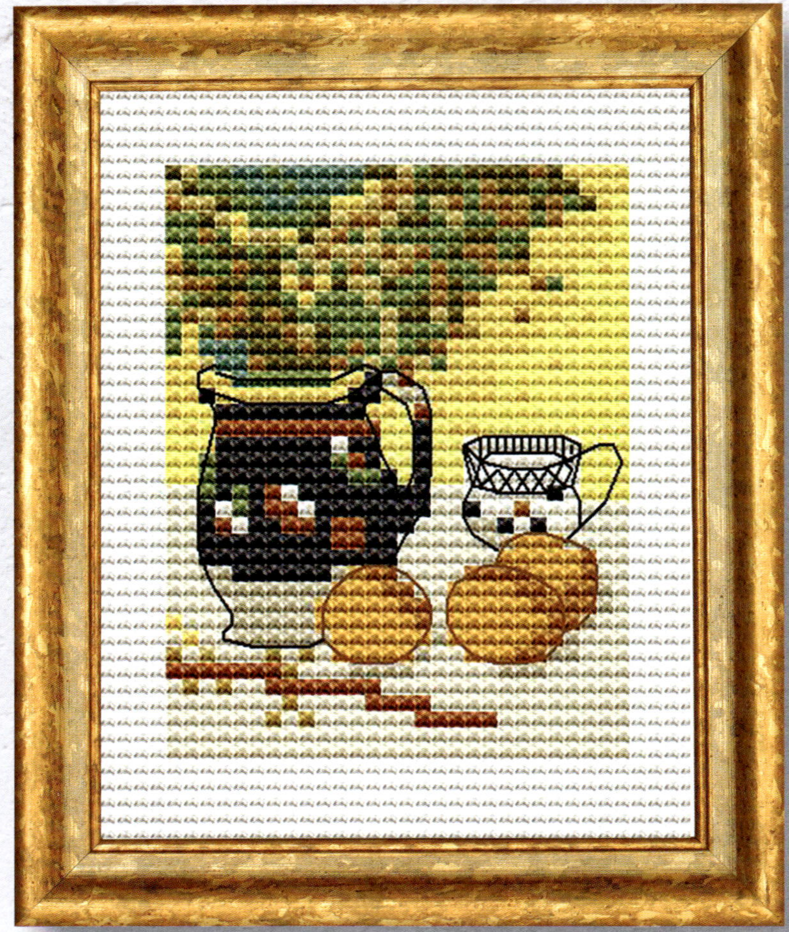

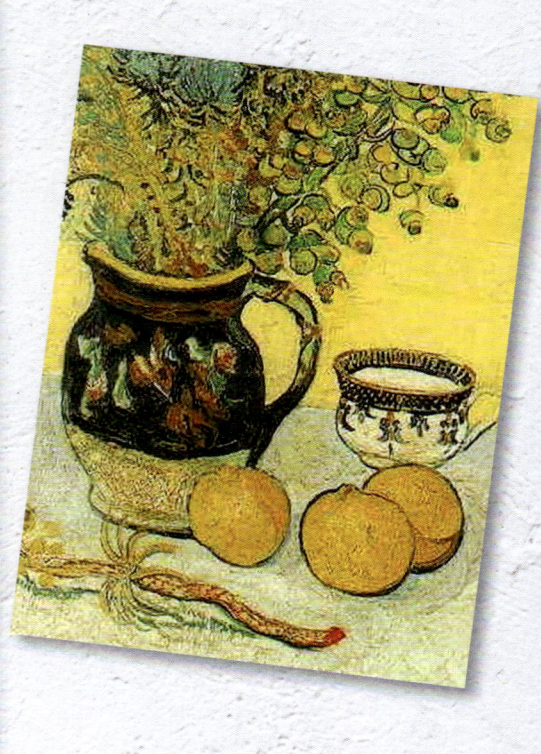

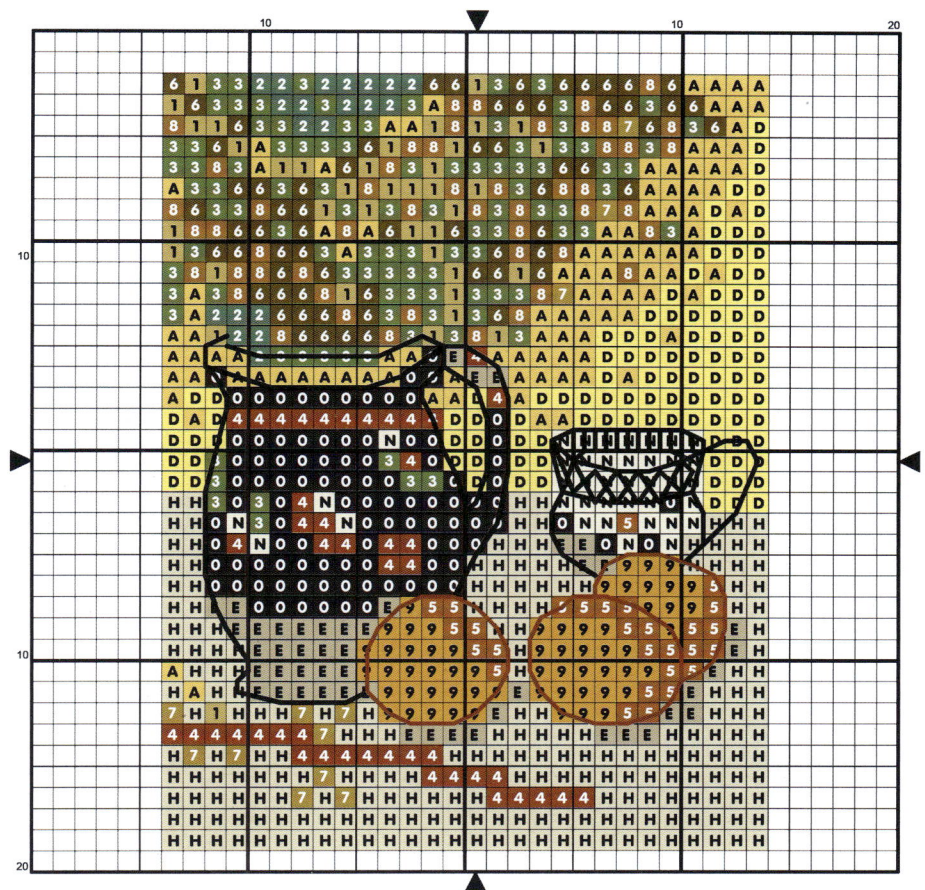

Symbol	Number	Color Name	Symbol	Number	Color Name
O	3799	Anthracite	3	3347	Asparagus
2	3816	Serpent	5	782	Wicker
4	3826	Fox	7	833	Brass
6	732	Light Bronzed Green	9	3820	Sunshine
8	680	Fennec	D	727	Primrose
A	3822	Corn Husk	H	822	Cotton
E	644	Hemp	▬	310	Metallic Black
N	712	Cream	▬	780	Chestnut
1	3046	Biscuit			

Vincent van Gogh

Sunflowers

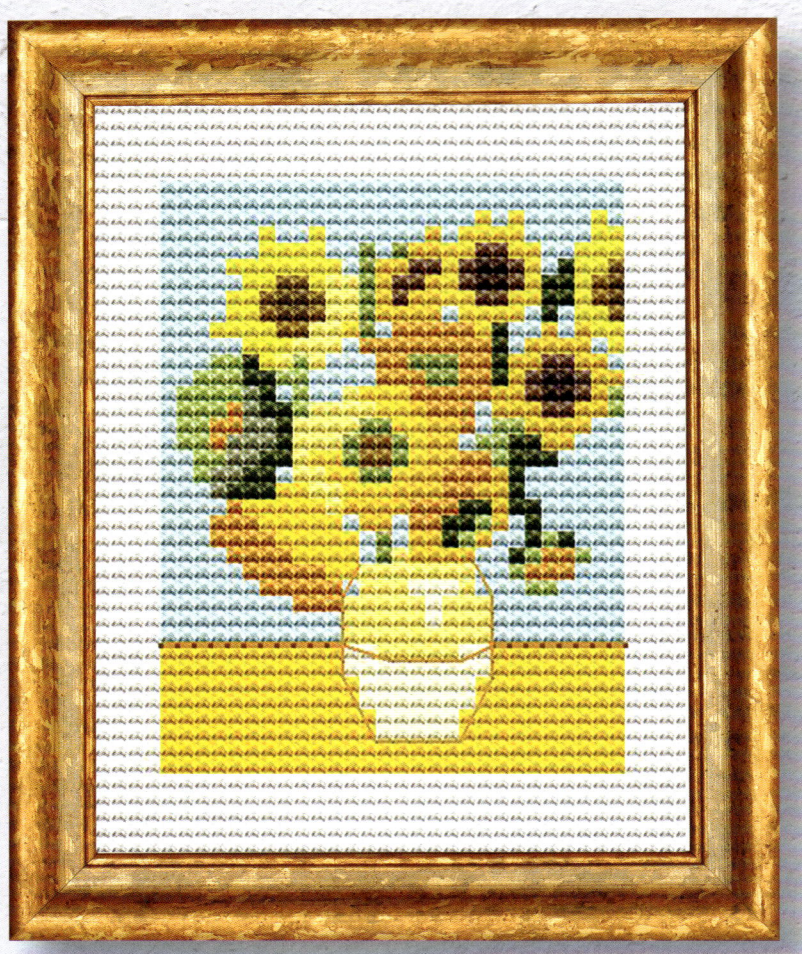
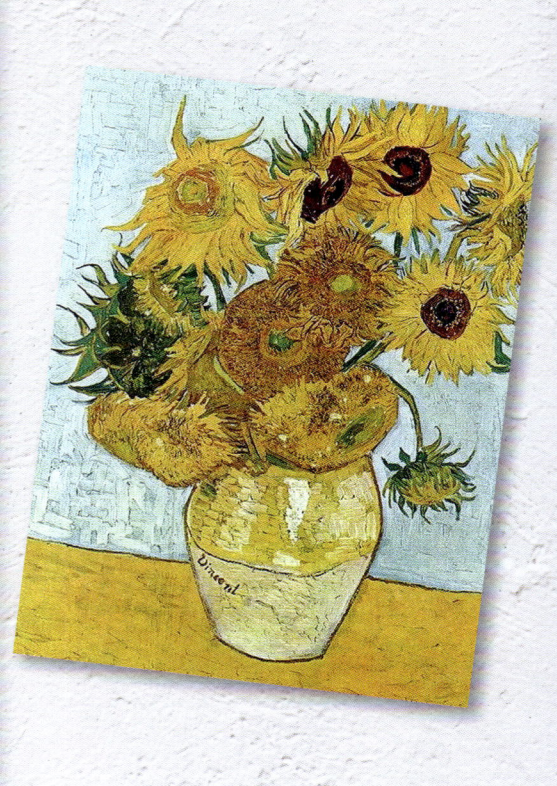
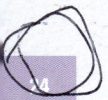

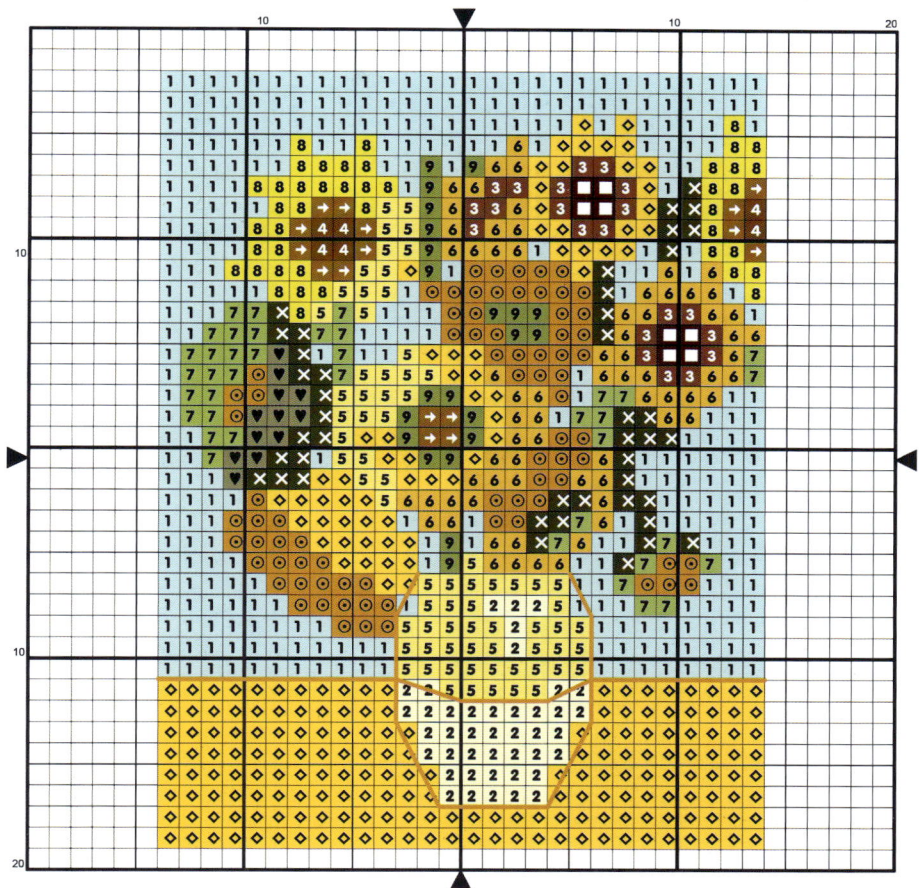

Symbol	Number	Color Name	Symbol	Number	Color Name
□	838	Dark Wood	✖	937	Moss
♥	523	Green Ash	⊙	3820	Sunshine
➔	832	Modoré	◇	973	Daffodil
1	747	Pearlescent Blue Sea Mist	2	746	Pearlescent Vanilla
3	840	Country Mouse	4	831	Bronze
5	727	Primrose	6	444	Bright Yellow
7	3348	Scallion	8	307	Lemon
9	471	Tarragon	—	3820	Sunshine

Vincent van Gogh

Three Sunflowers

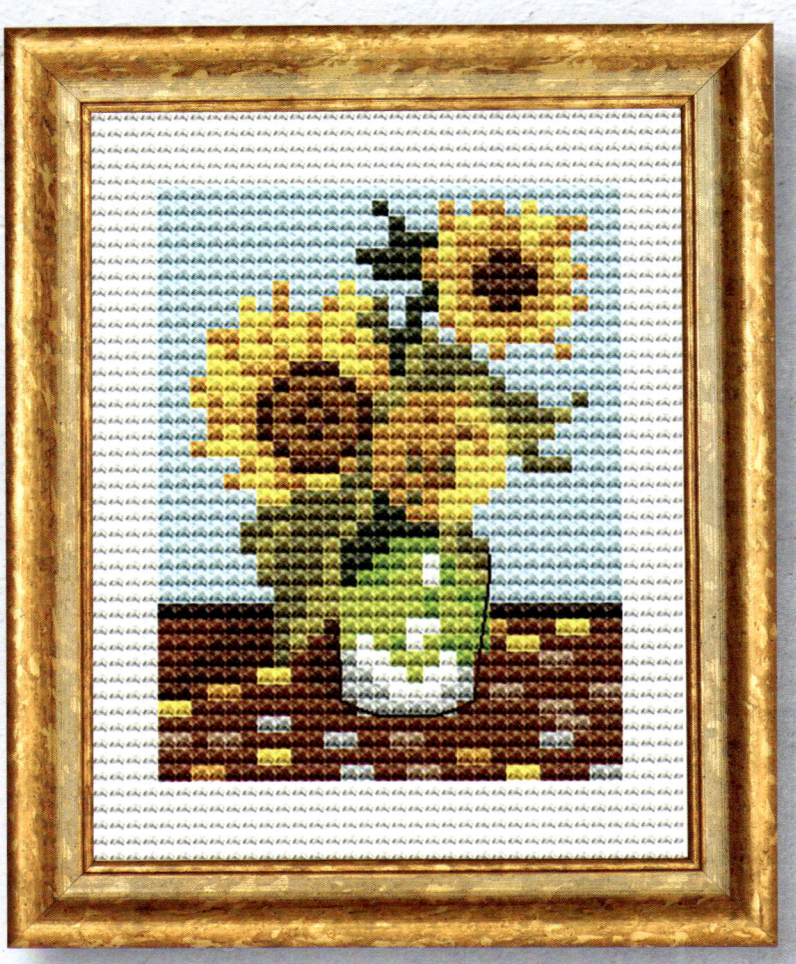
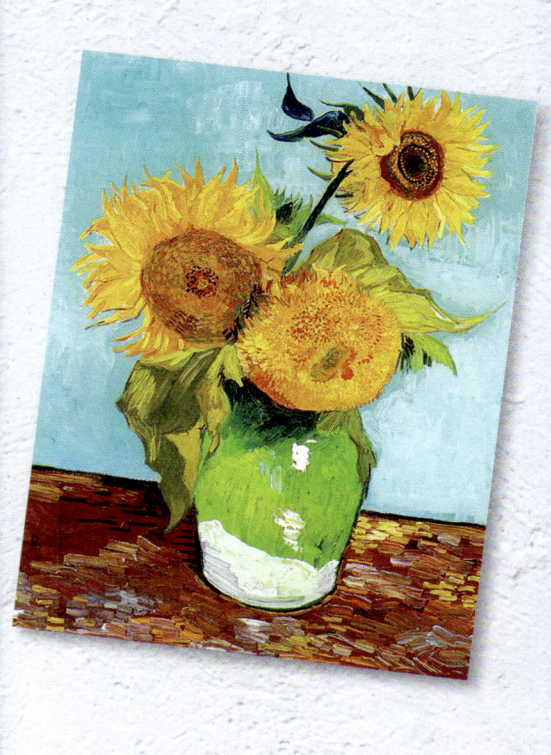

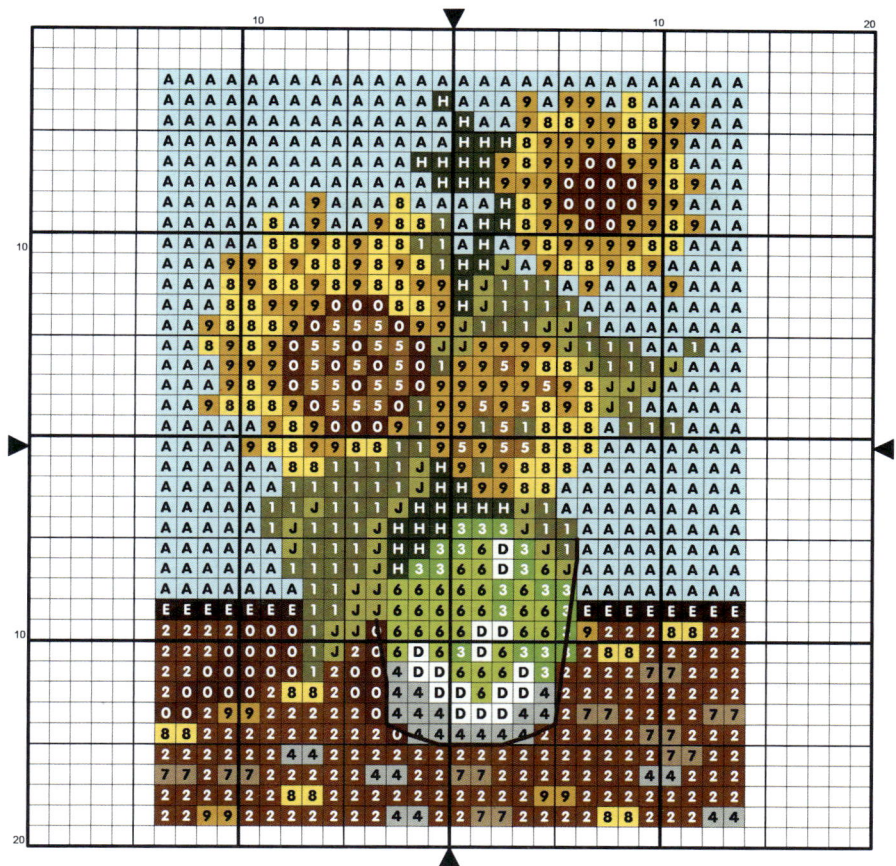

Symbol	Number	Color Name	Symbol	Number	Color Name
0	433	Chocolate	1	3012	Dried Moss
2	434	Cigar Brown	3	907	Granny Smith
4	928	Oyster Shell	5	3829	Ochre Earth
6	3819	Aurous Green	7	3864	Vicuna Wool
8	726	Mimosa	9	3820	Sunshine
A	747	Pearlescent Blue Sea Mist	D	3865	Edelweiss
E	938	Clove	H	3051	Forest Green
J	734	Broken Olive	—	938	Clove

Vincent van Gogh

Vase of Roses

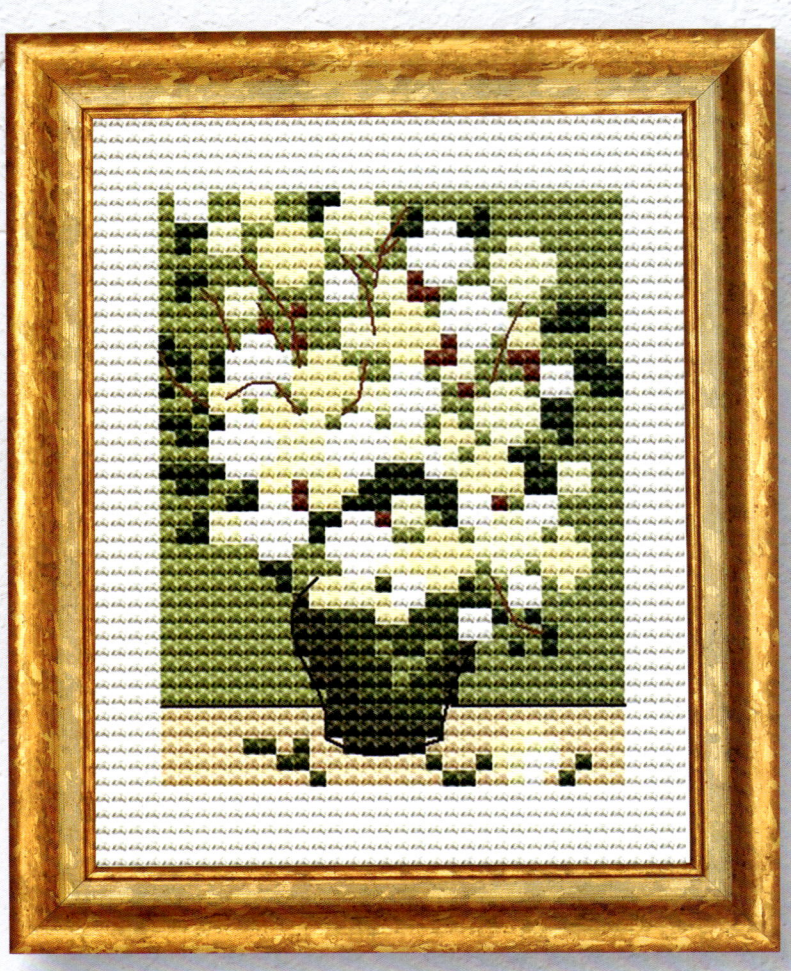
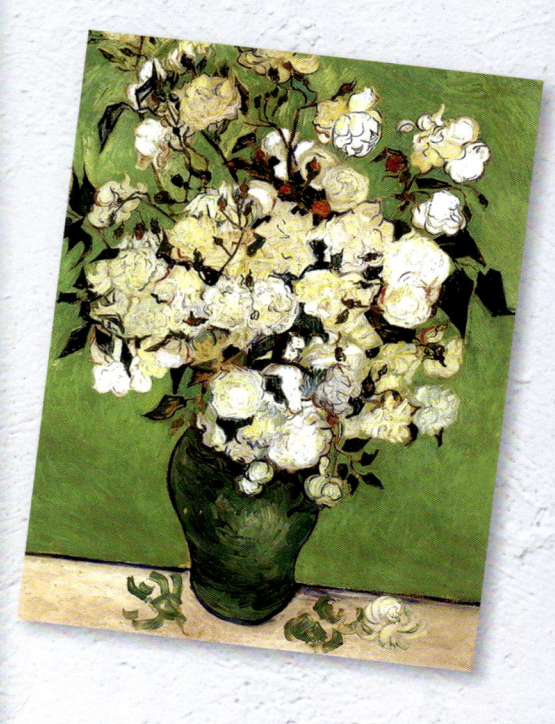

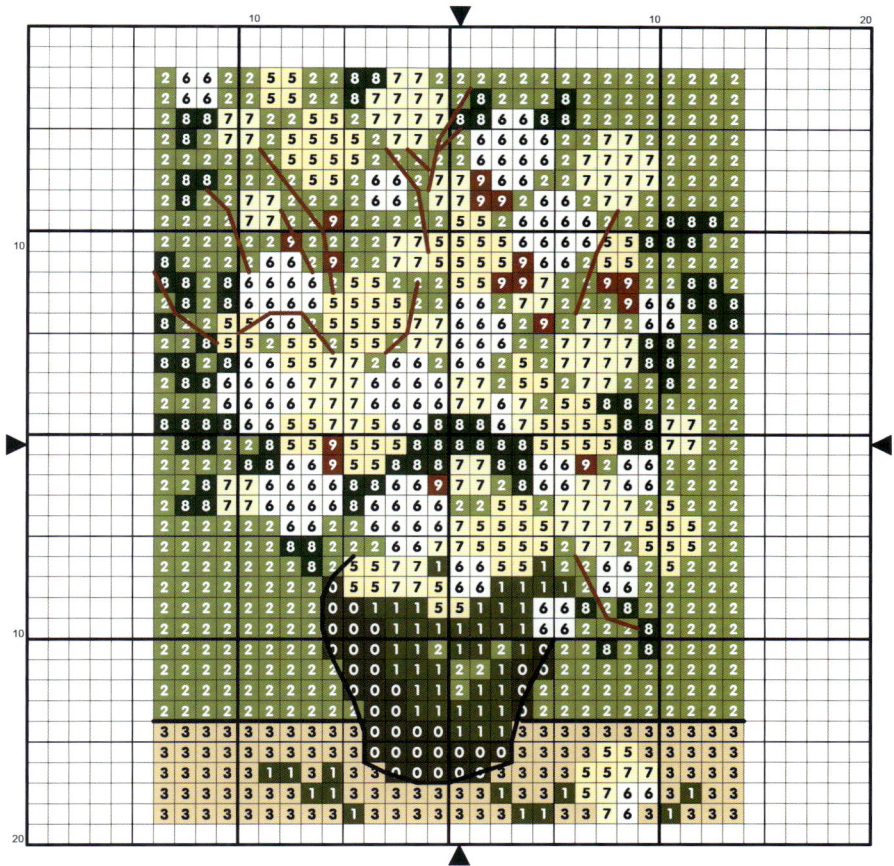

Symbol	Number	Color Name	Symbol	Number	Color Name
0	935	Undergrowth	3	739	Dune
2	3364	Sage	6	3865	Edelweiss
5	3823	Moonshine	8	895	Bottle Green
7	746	Pearlescent Vanilla	—	310	Metallic Black
9	632	Cocoa	—	632	Cocoa
1	937	Moss			

Vincent van Gogh

Vase with Carnations

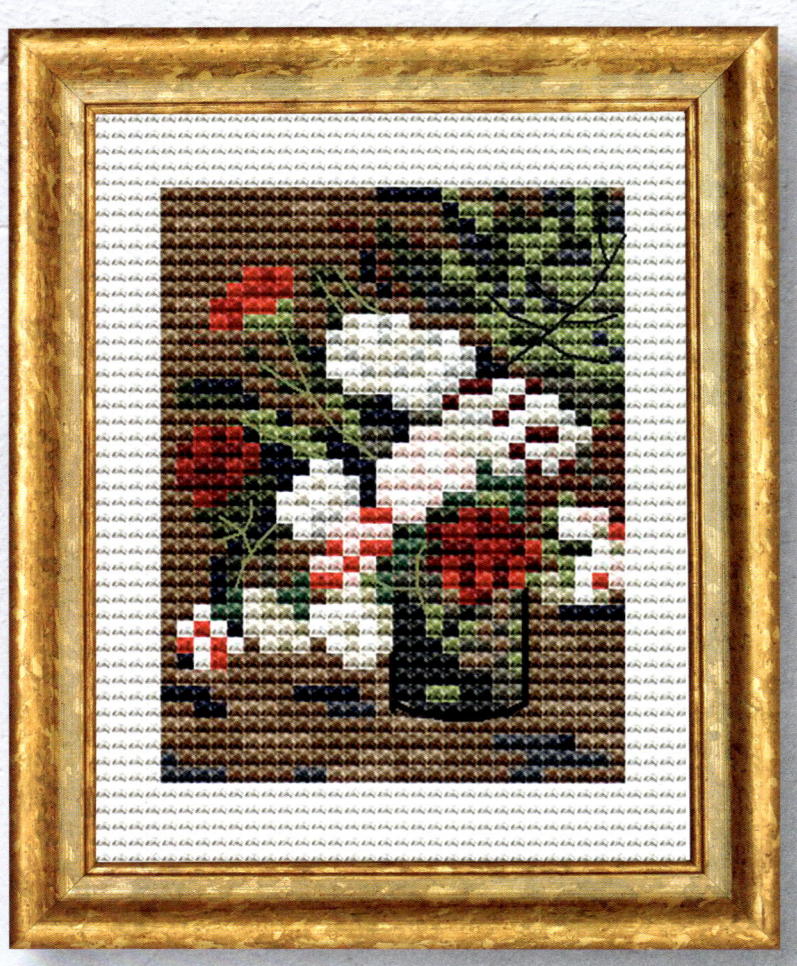
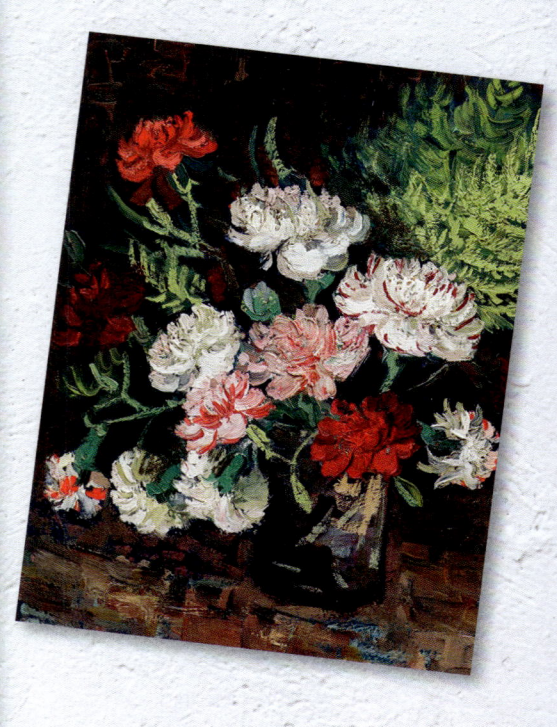

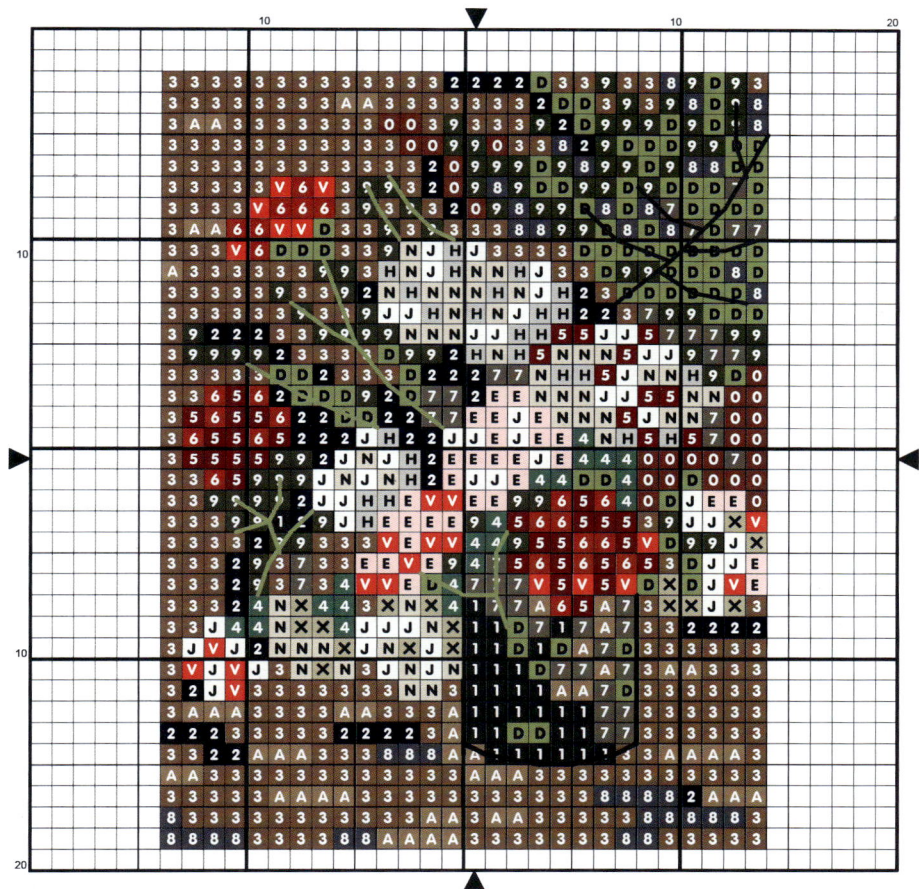

Symbol	Number	Color Name	Symbol	Number	Color Name
O	3858	Rose Brown	5	815	Metallic Black Cherry
2	823	Blueberry	7	646	Smoke Grey
4	163	Eucalyptus	9	3362	Conifer
6	321	Metallic Carmine Red	D	3364	Sage
8	317	Metallic Steel	H	3072	Thunderous Skies
A	841	Suede	N	3866	Garlic White
E	818	Pearlescent Powder Pink	X	644	Hemp
J	3865	Edelweiss	———	3799	Anthracite
V	3801	Tulip Red	———	3364	Sage
1	3799	Anthracite	———	310	Metallic Black
3	840	Country Mouse			

Vincent van Gogh

Vase with Oleanders and Books

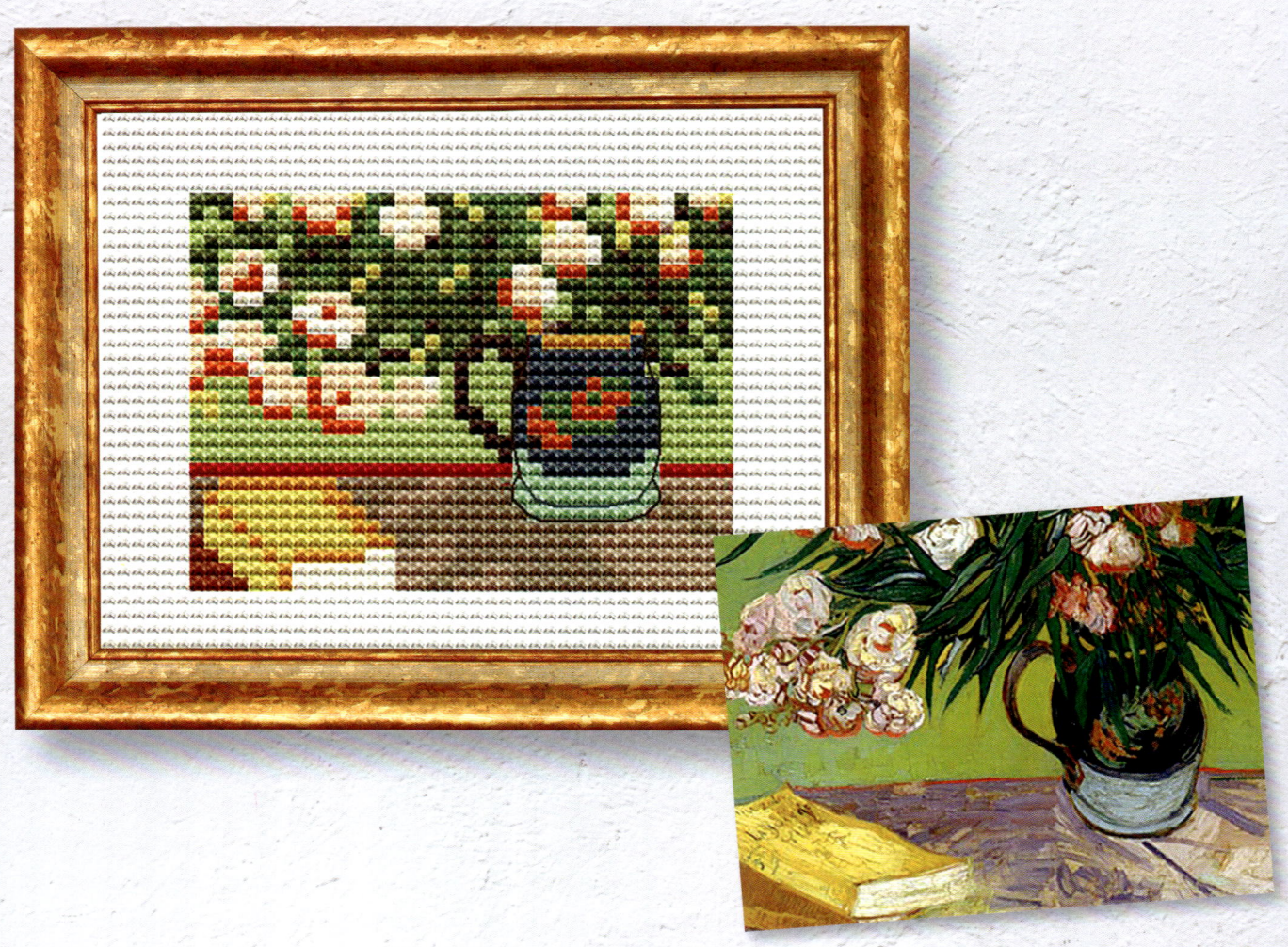

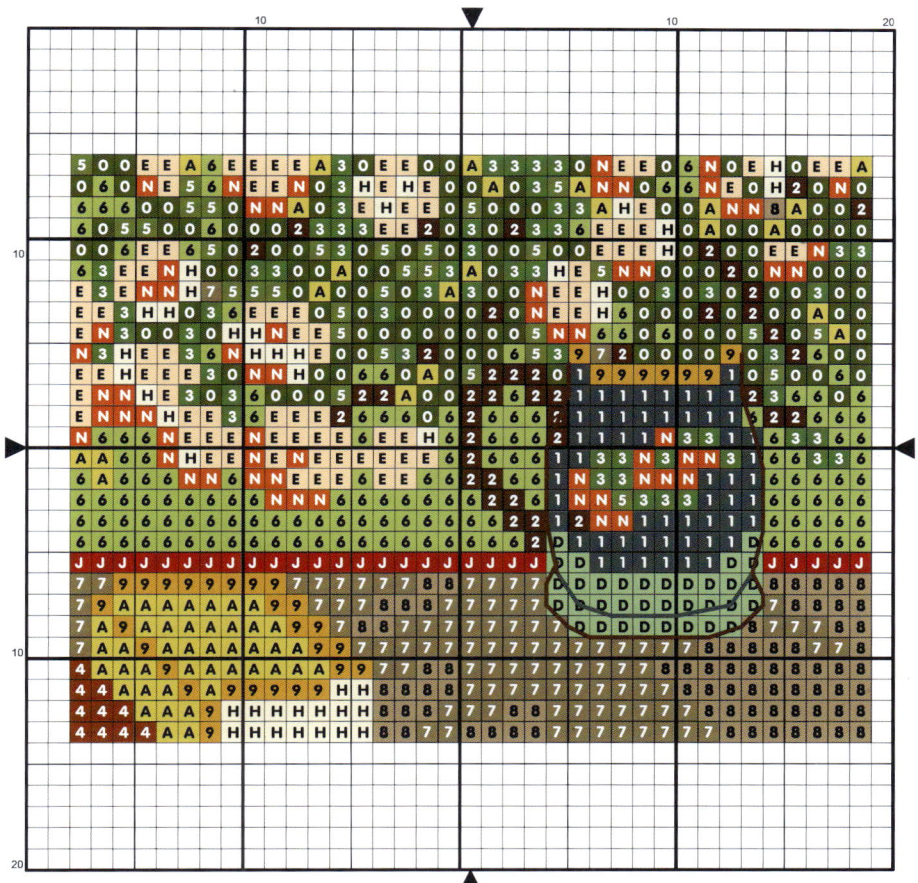

Symbol	Number	Color Name	Symbol	Number	Color Name
O	3346	Artichoke	3	988	Verbena Stem
2	3021	Ink	5	3347	Asparagus
4	780	Chestnut	7	642	Umbra Grey
6	3348	Scallion	9	3820	Sunshine
8	3782	Ginger	D	966	Pearlescent Soft Green
A	17	Maize	H	712	Cream
E	951	Cashmere Beige	N	3853	Copper
J	321	Metallic Carmine Red		3768	Storm
1	3768	Storm		3021	Ink

Vincent van Gogh

Vase with Poppies

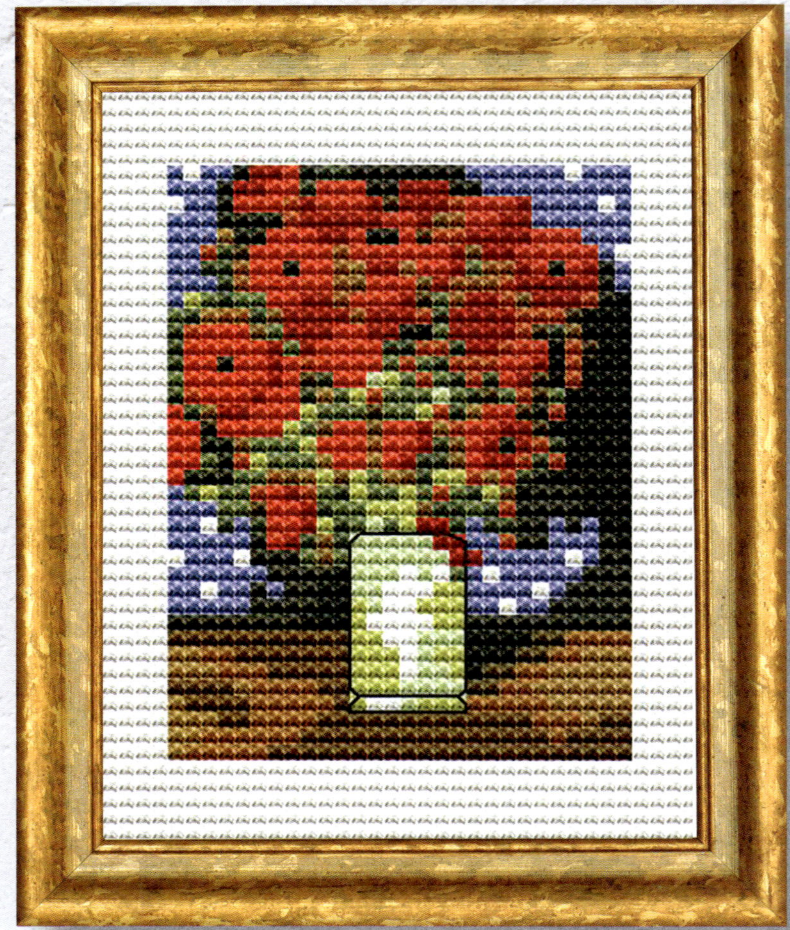

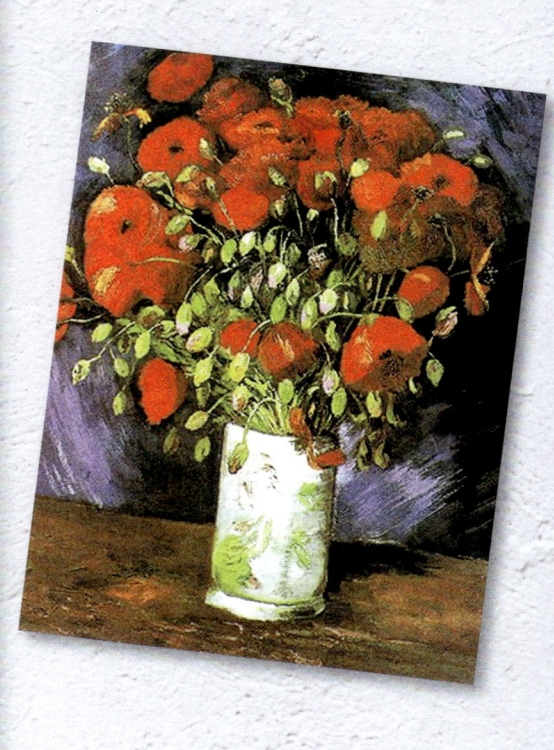

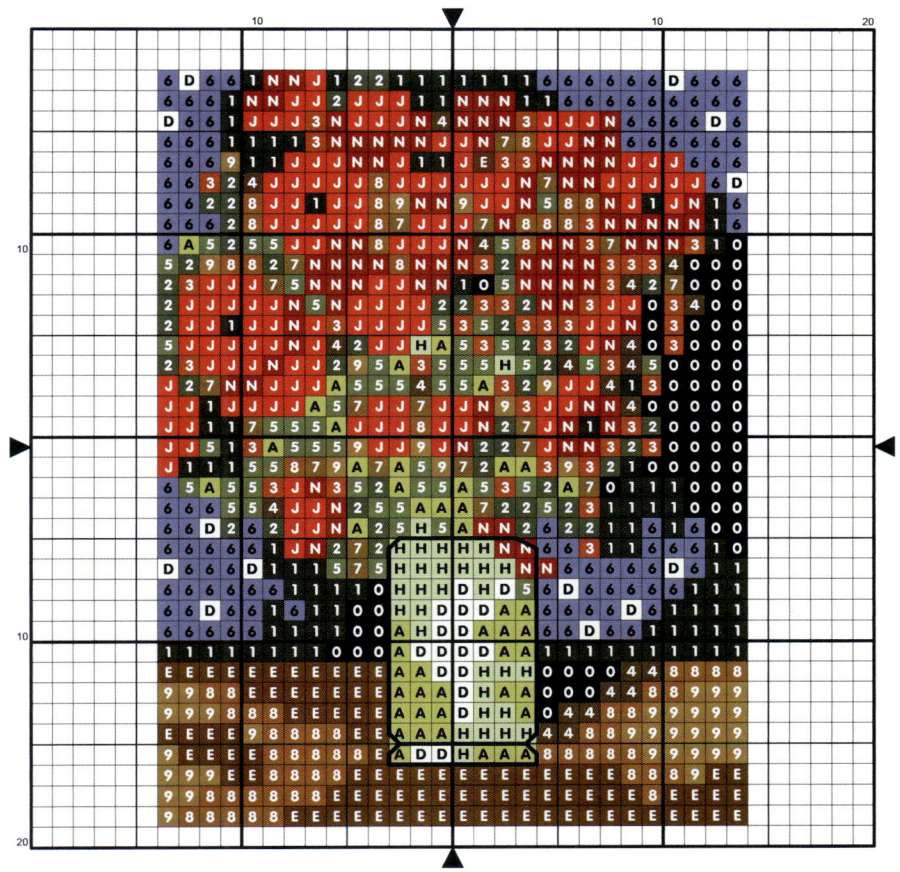

Symbol	Number	Color Name	Symbol	Number	Color Name
0	310	Metallic Black	3	921	Tuscan Ochre
2	645	Reindeer Grey	5	3052	Silver Green
4	610	Beaver	7	167	Praline
6	156	Cornflower Blue	9	3828	Oak
8	435	Tobacco	D	3865	Edelweiss
A	472	Green Bud	H	369	Bamboo Shoot Green
E	869	Coffee	N	817	Japanese Red
J	350	Vermillion		310	Metallic Black
1	844	Black Pepper			

William Harnett

The Old Violin

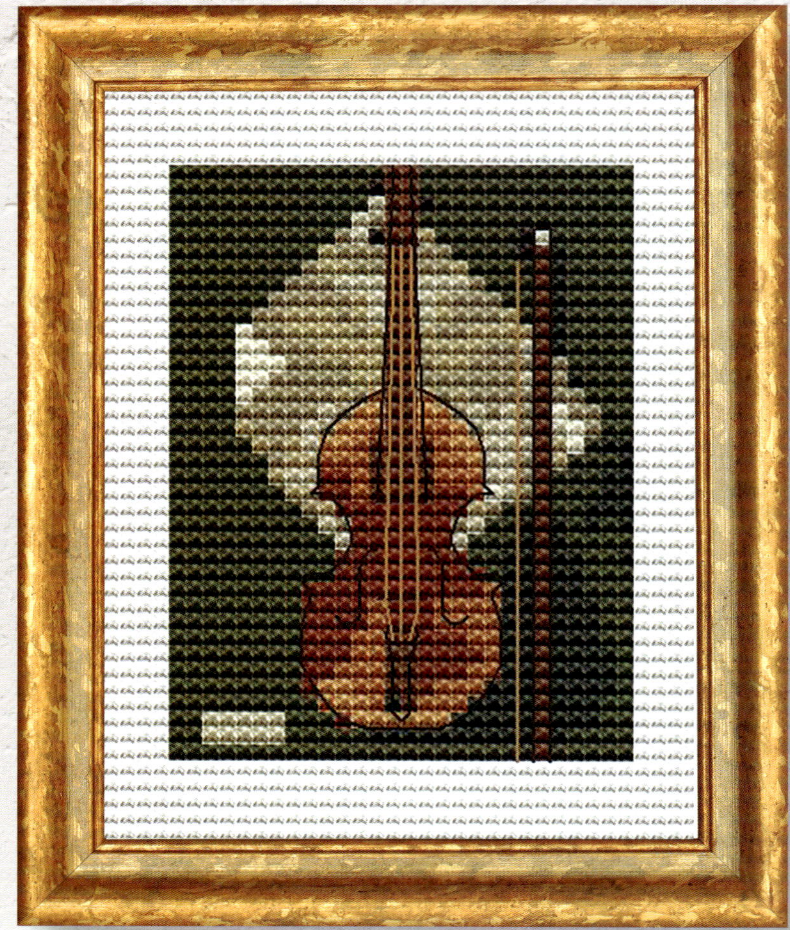

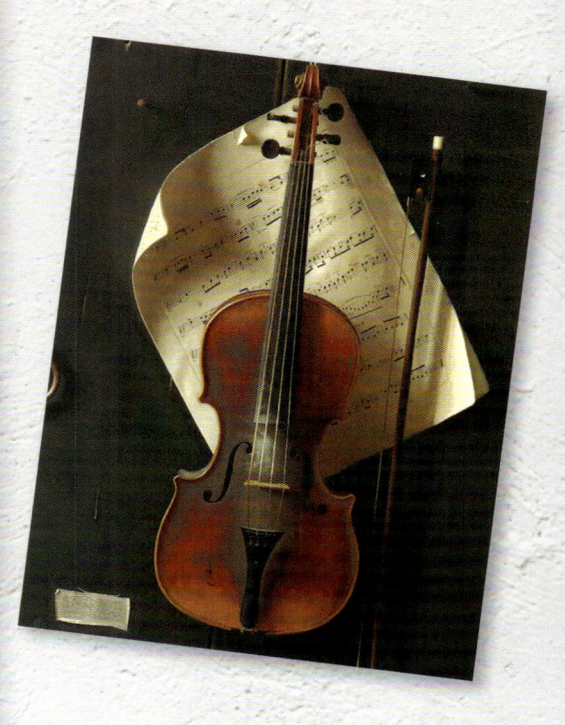

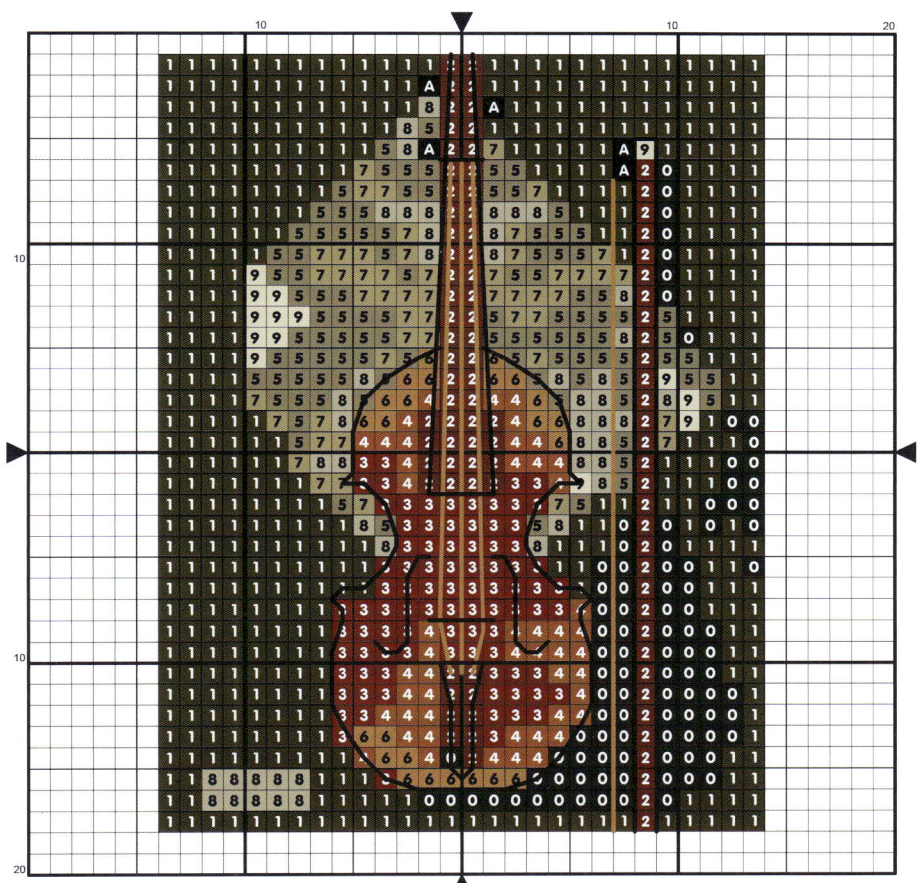

Symbol	Number	Color Name	Symbol	Number	Color Name
0	934	Seaweed	3	400	Conker
2	433	Chocolate	5	3032	Stone
4	435	Tobacco	7	613	Twine
6	436	Metallic Teddy	9	822	Cotton
8	644	Hemp	—	436	Metallic Teddy
A	3371	Peppercorn	—	3371	Peppercorn
1	936	Oak Moss			

Shirley Hibberd

Various Ivy Leaves

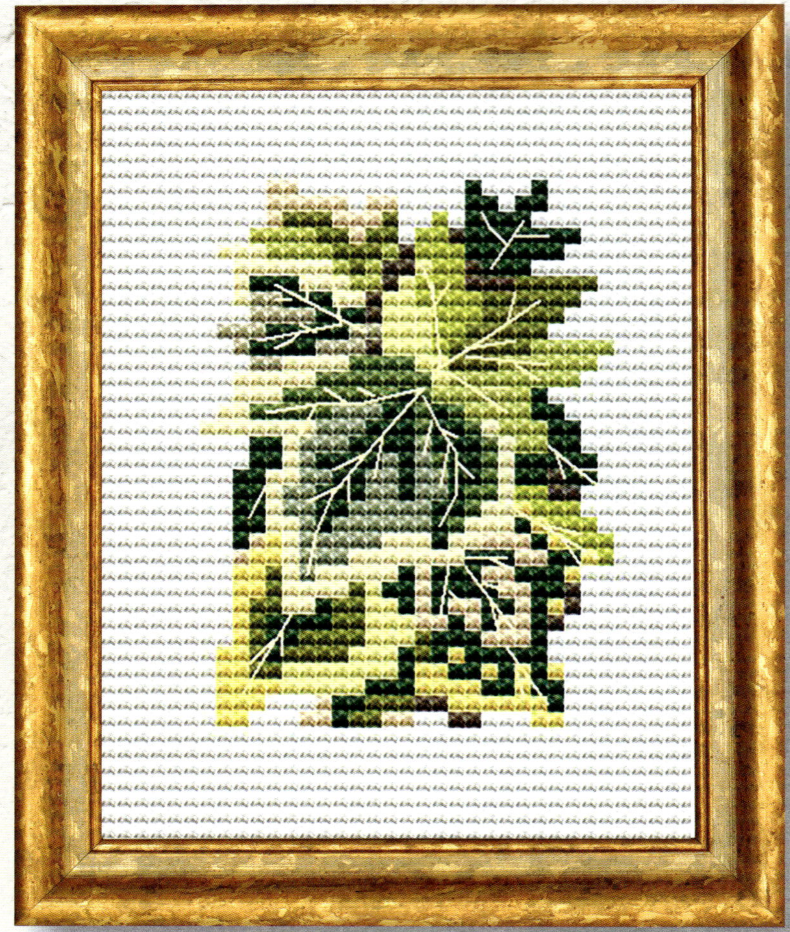

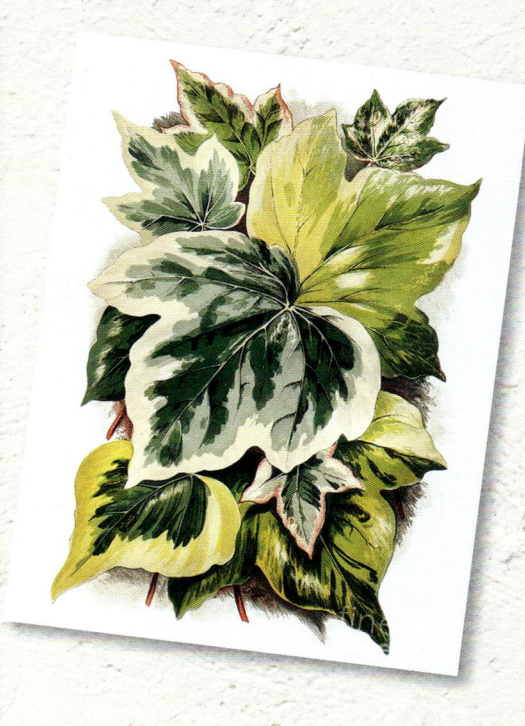

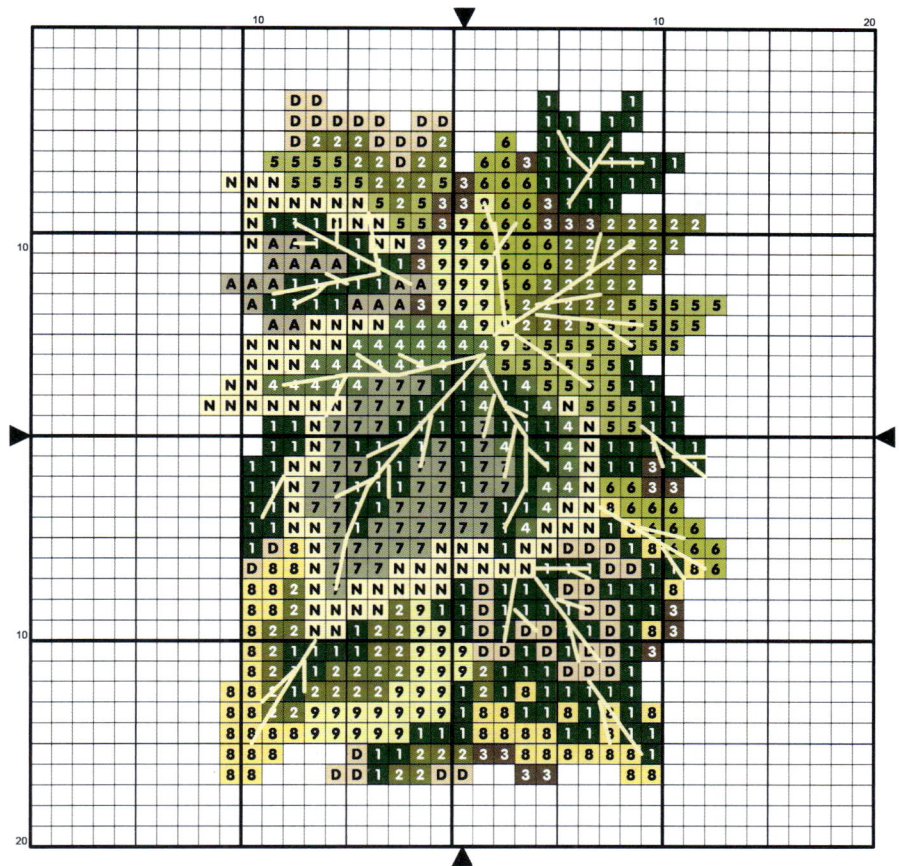

Symbol	Number	Color Name	Symbol	Number	Color Name
1	986	Boxwood	4	3347	Asparagus
3	08	Racoon	6	3819	Aurous Green
5	472	Green Bud	8	744	Grapefruit
7	524	Pebble Green	A	644	Hemp
9	3078	Buttermilk	N	3823	Moonshine
D	739	Dune		3823	Moonshine
2	581	Grasshopper			

Nora Heysen

Spring Flowers

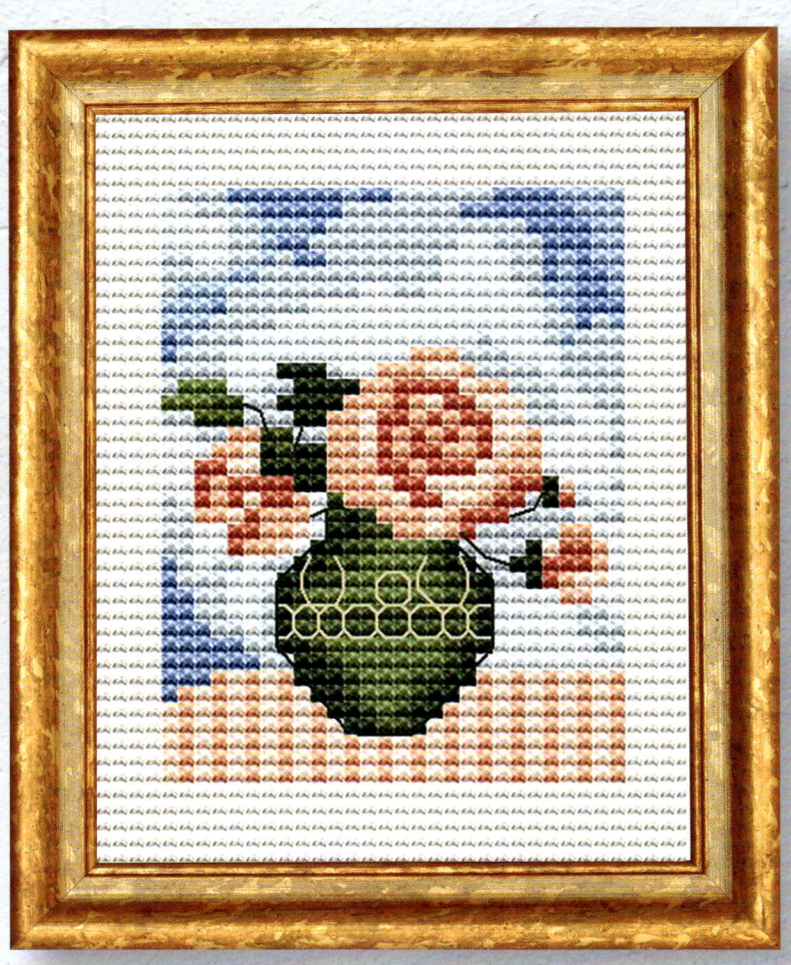
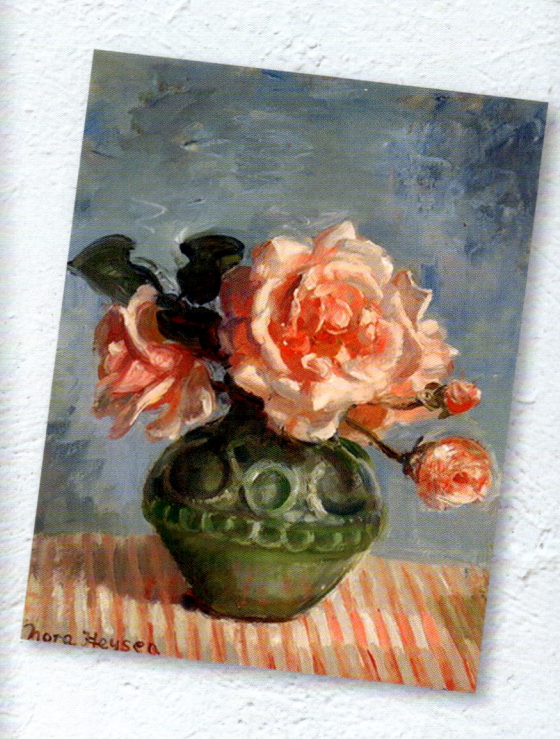

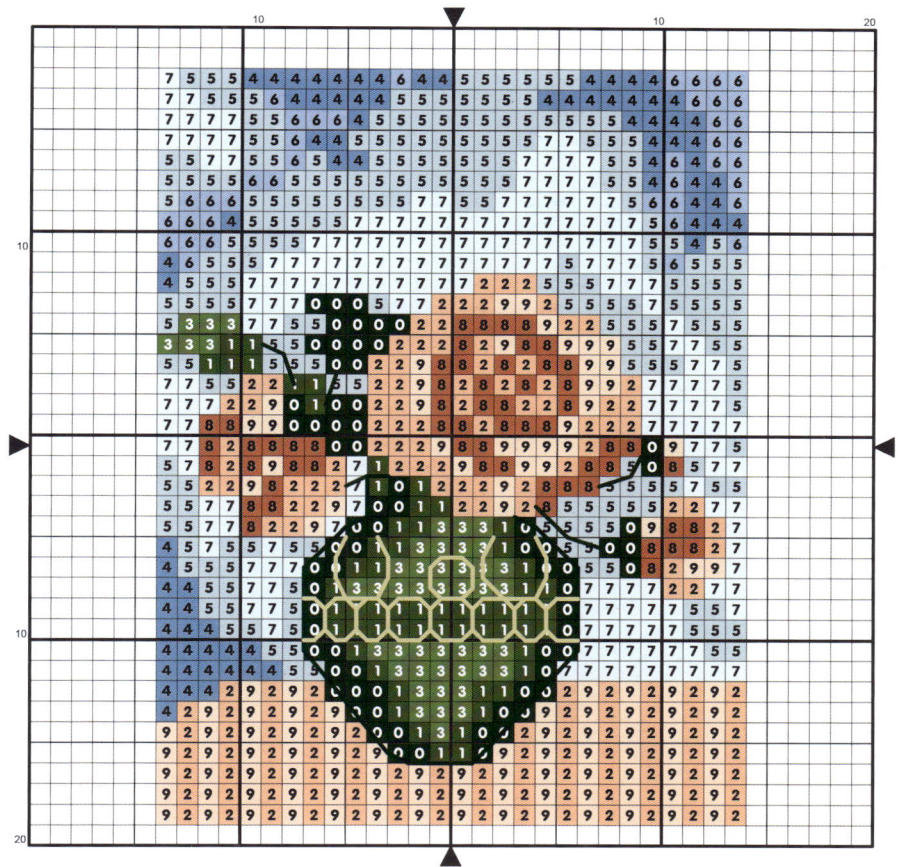

Symbol	Number	Color Name	Symbol	Number	Color Name
0	895	Bottle Green	5	775	Blue Summer Rain
2	754	Beige Rose	7	3756	Cloud Blue
4	3755	Pastel Blue	9	948	Himalayan Salt
6	3325	Arctic Blue	—	895	Bottle Green
8	3778	Rose Gold	—	890	Black Forest
1	3346	Artichoke	—	3047	Sawdust
3	3347	Asparagus			

Michiel van Huysum

Branch with a Sunflower

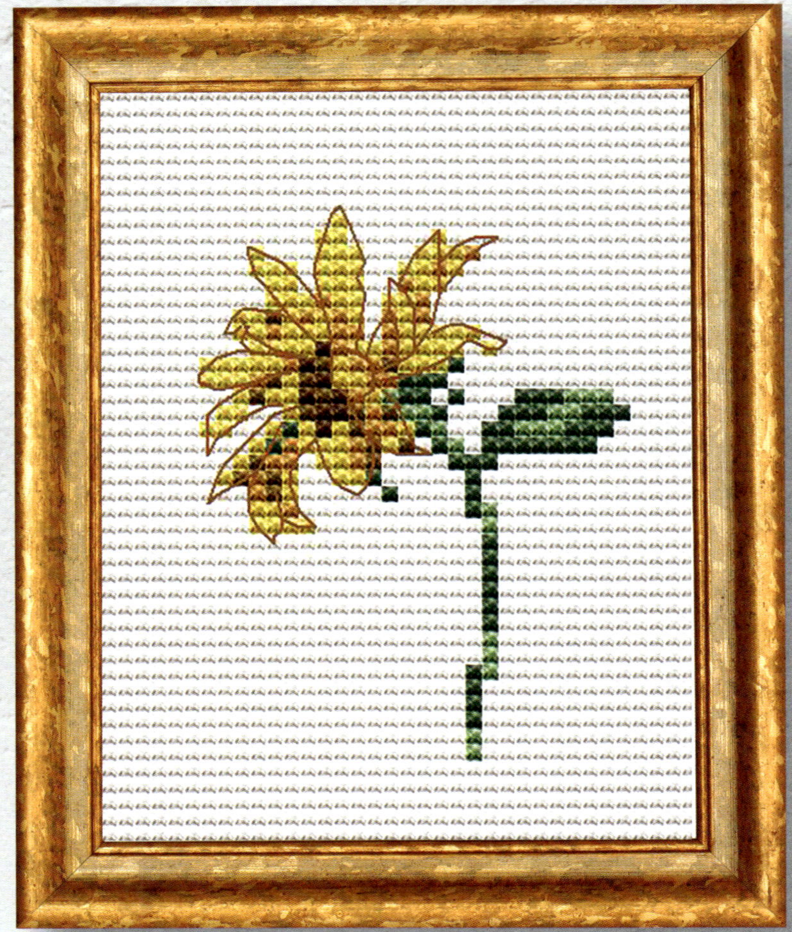

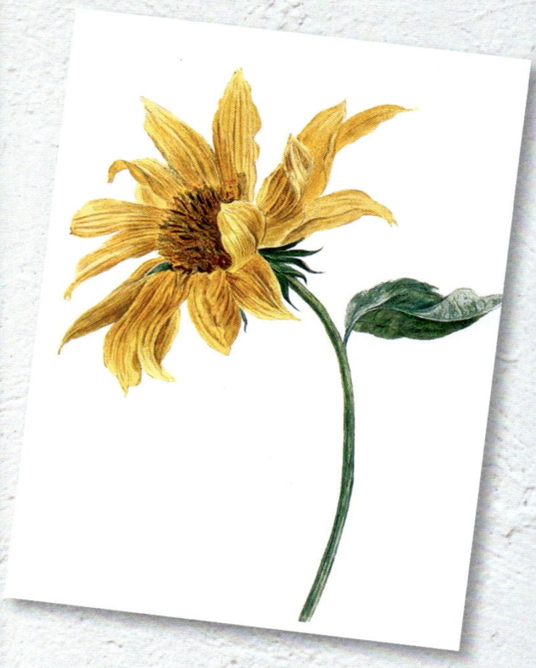

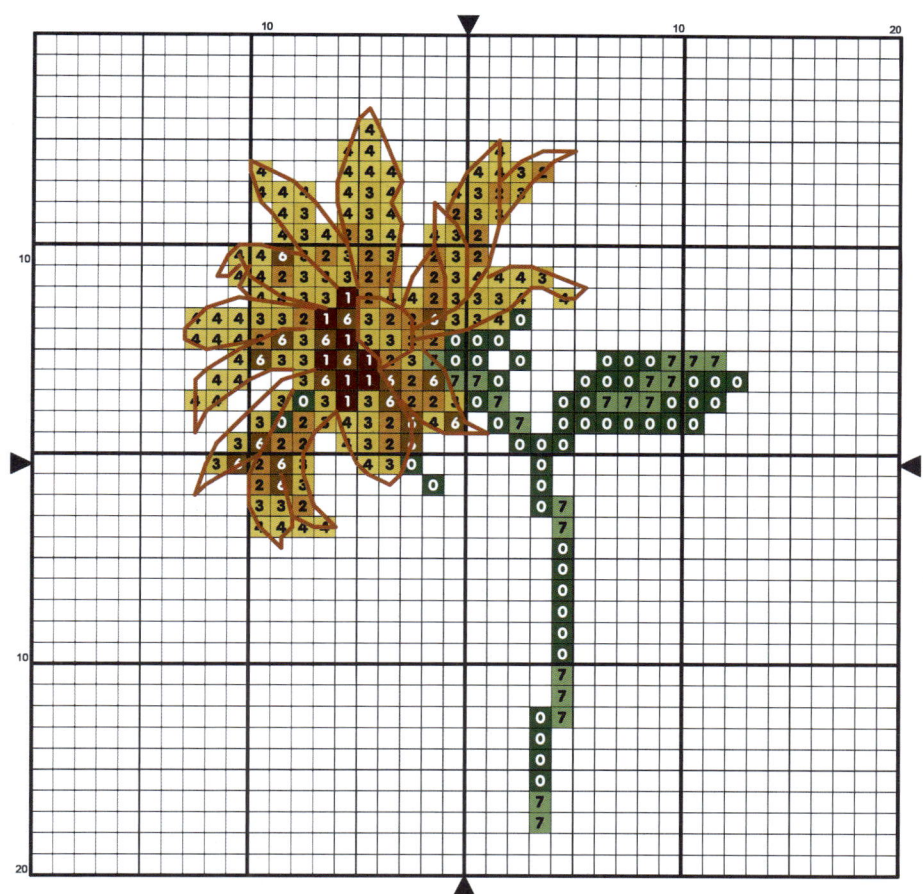

Symbol	Number	Color Name	Symbol	Number	Color Name
o	367	Laurel	1	801	Mink
2	729	Honey	3	18	Corn
4	17	Maize	6	831	Bronze
7	368	Eau de Nile	—	435	Tobacco

Jan van Kessel

Vanitas Still Life

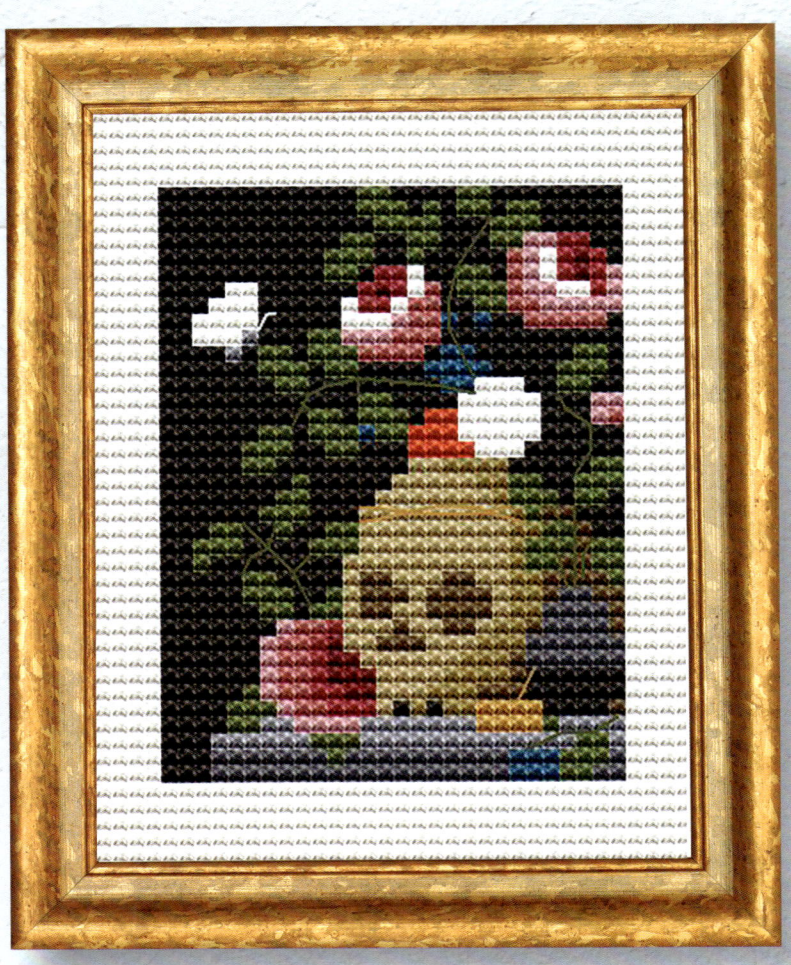
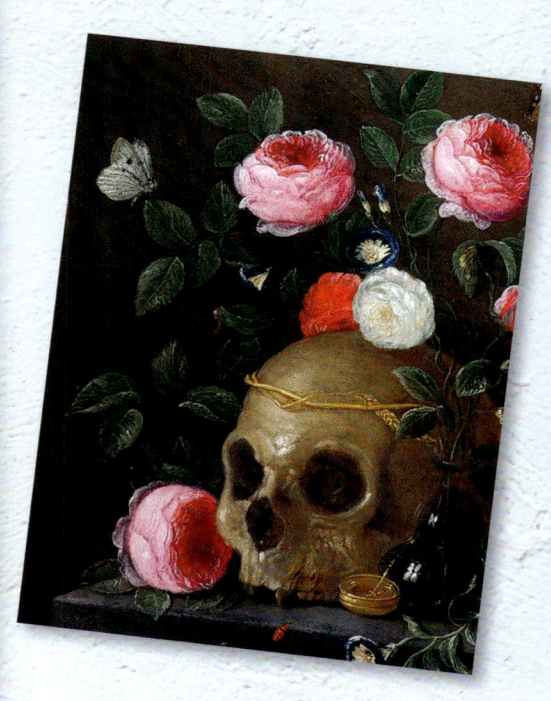

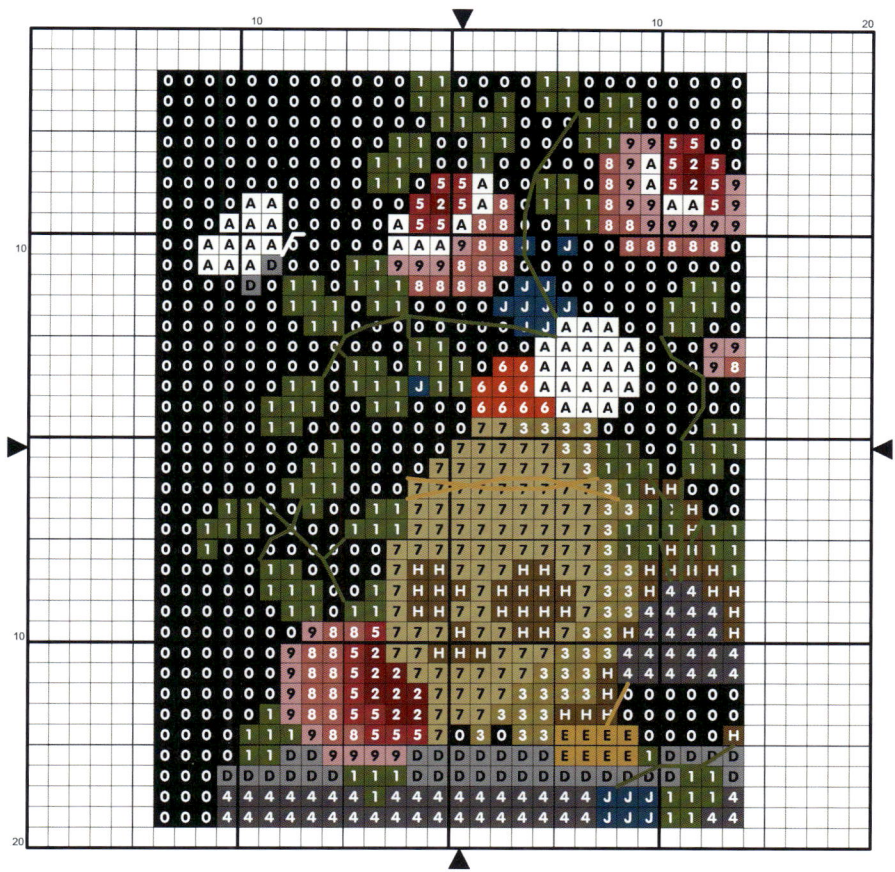

Symbol	Number	Color Name	Symbol	Number	Color Name
0	310	Metallic Black	3	371	Steppe
2	815	Metallic Black Cherry	5	3350	Dragonfruit
4	317	Metallic Steel	7	613	Twine
6	900	Blood Orange	9	3727	Lycee
8	223	Granite Pink	D	318	Granite Grey
A	3865	Edelweiss	H	610	Beaver
E	729	Honey		3346	Artichoke
J	3765	Blue Teal		3865	Edelweiss
1	3346	Artichoke		729	Honey

August Macke

The Ghost in the House Stalls–Still Life with a Cat

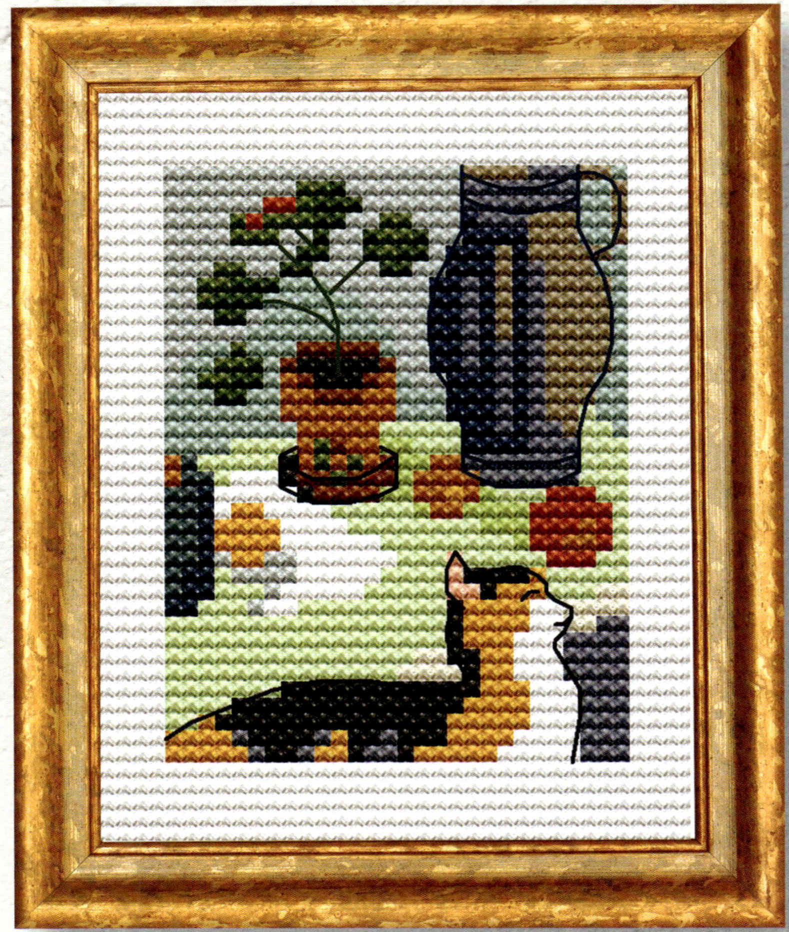

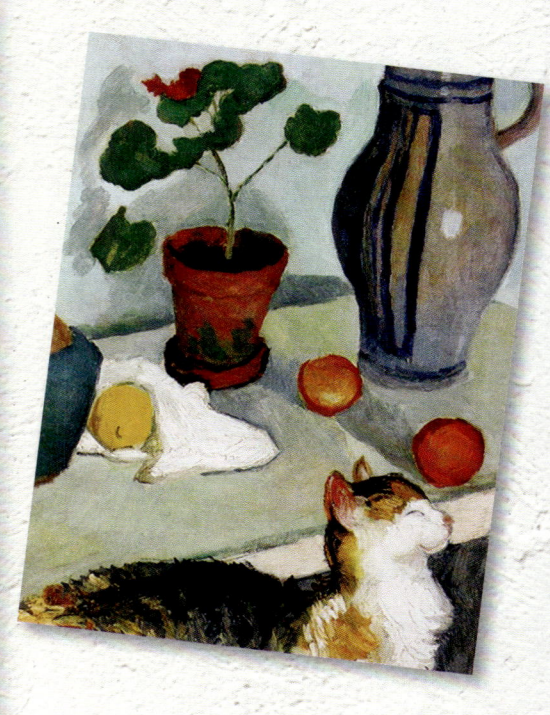

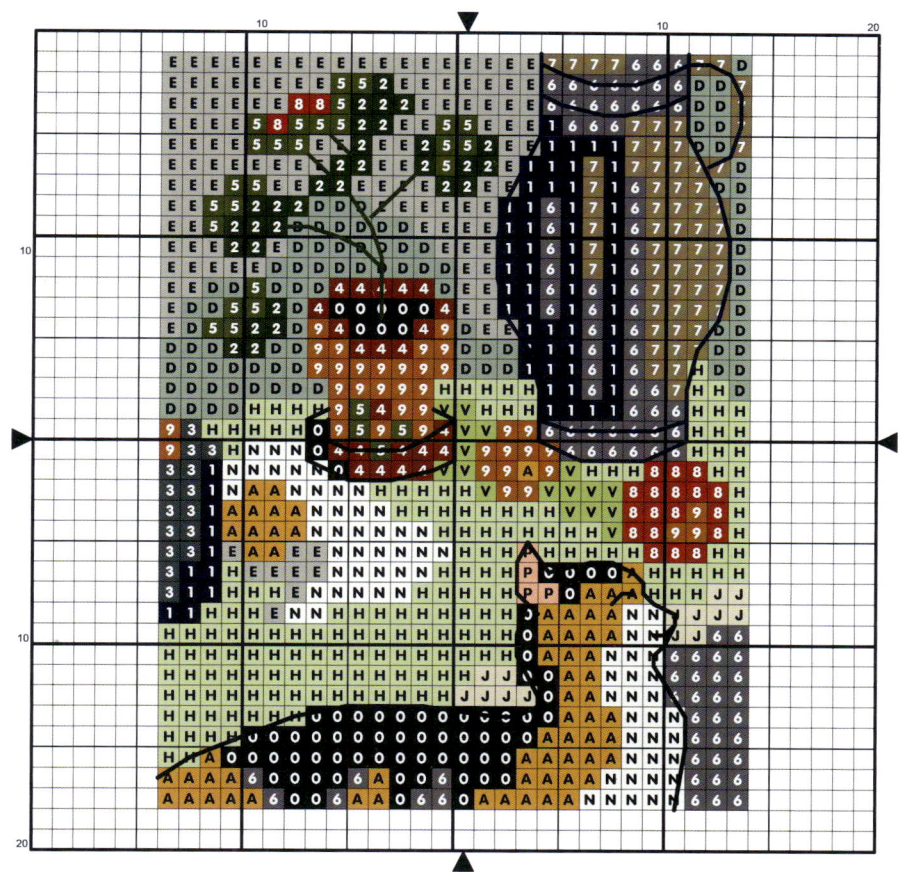

Symbol	Number	Color Name	Symbol	Number	Color Name
0	310	Metallic Black	5	3346	Artichoke
2	3345	Spinach	7	642	Umbra Grey
4	975	Weasel	9	782	Wicker
6	414	Lead	D	3813	Lichen Green
8	920	Sienna Ochre	H	369	Bamboo Shoot Green
A	3820	Sunshine	N	3865	Edelweiss
E	928	Oyster Shell	V	3348	Scallion
J	822	Cotton	——	310	Metallic Black
P	754	Beige Rose	——	3750	Dark Petrol Blue
1	3750	Dark Petrol Blue	——	3345	Spinach
3	3768	Storm			

August Macke

Little Walter's Toys

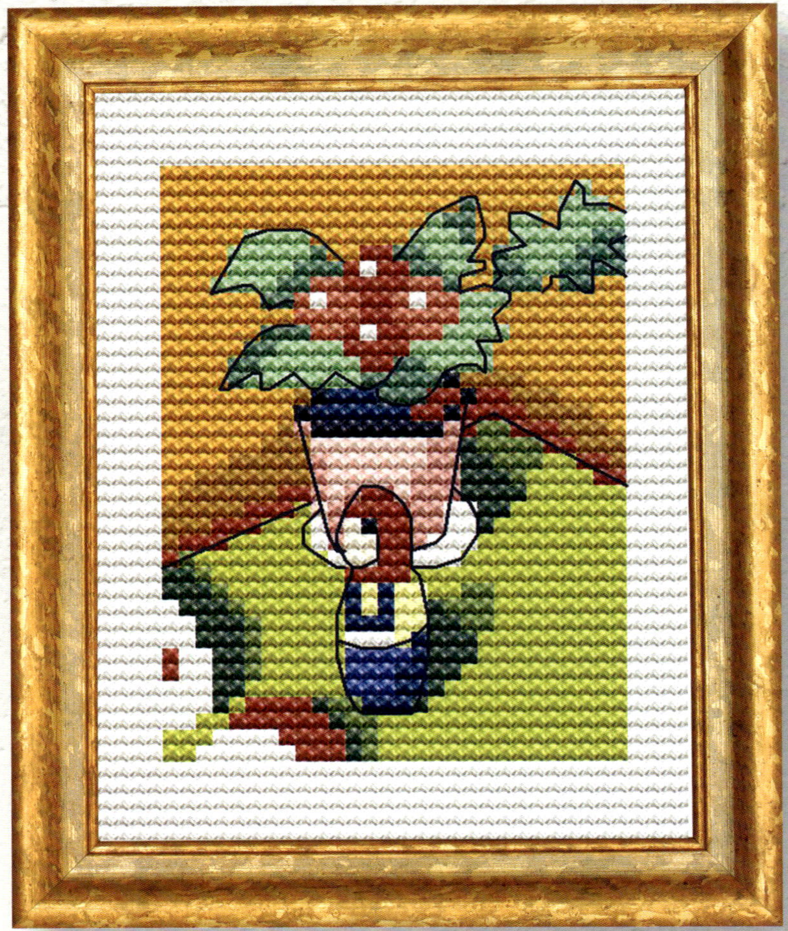

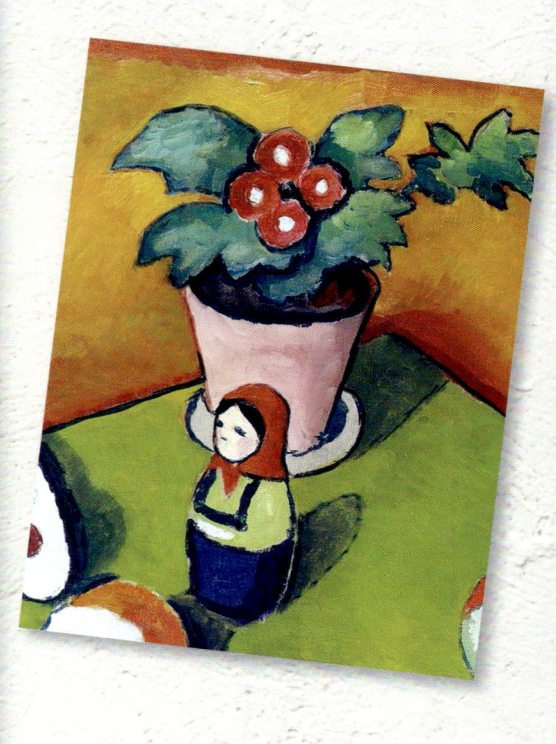

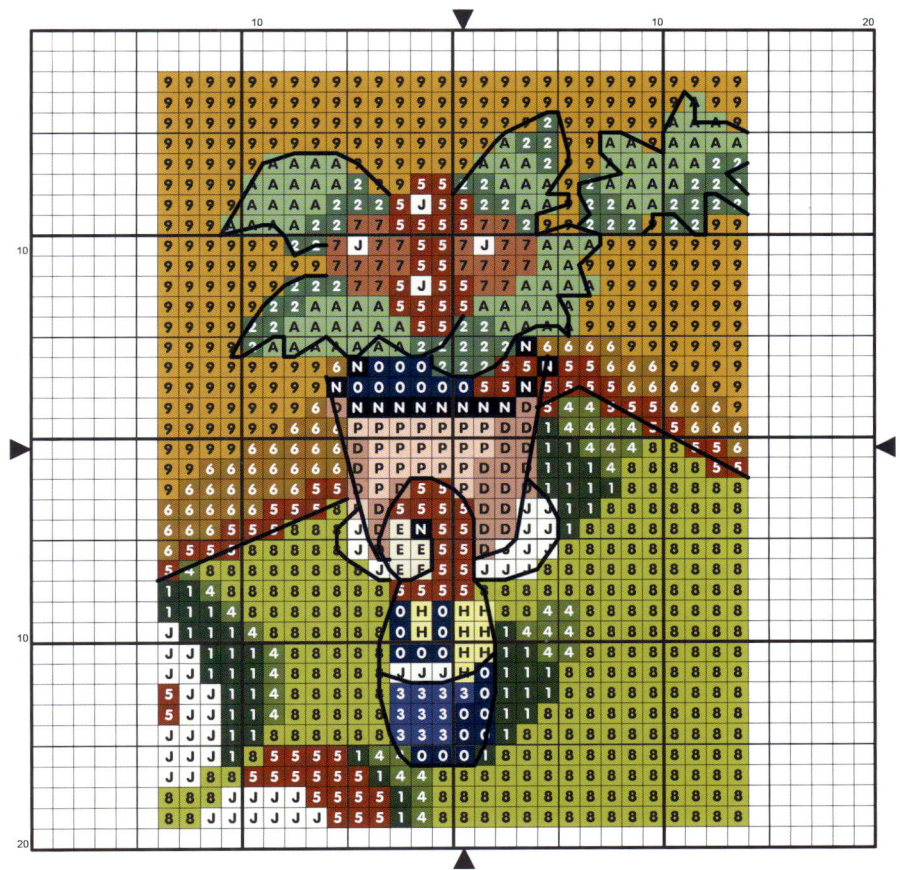

Symbol	Number	Color Name	Symbol	Number	Color Name
O	312	Midnight Blue	1	501	Pond Green
2	3816	Serpent	3	798	Cobalt Blue
4	3347	Asparagus	5	22	Ruby
6	680	Fennec	7	21	Prosciutto
8	3819	Aurous Green	9	3820	Sunshine
A	966	Pearlescent Soft Green	D	224	Earthworm
E	712	Cream	H	3078	Buttermilk
J	3865	Edelweiss	N	823	Blueberry
P	225	Cherry Blossom		823	Blueberry

Édouard Manet

Moss Roses in a Vase

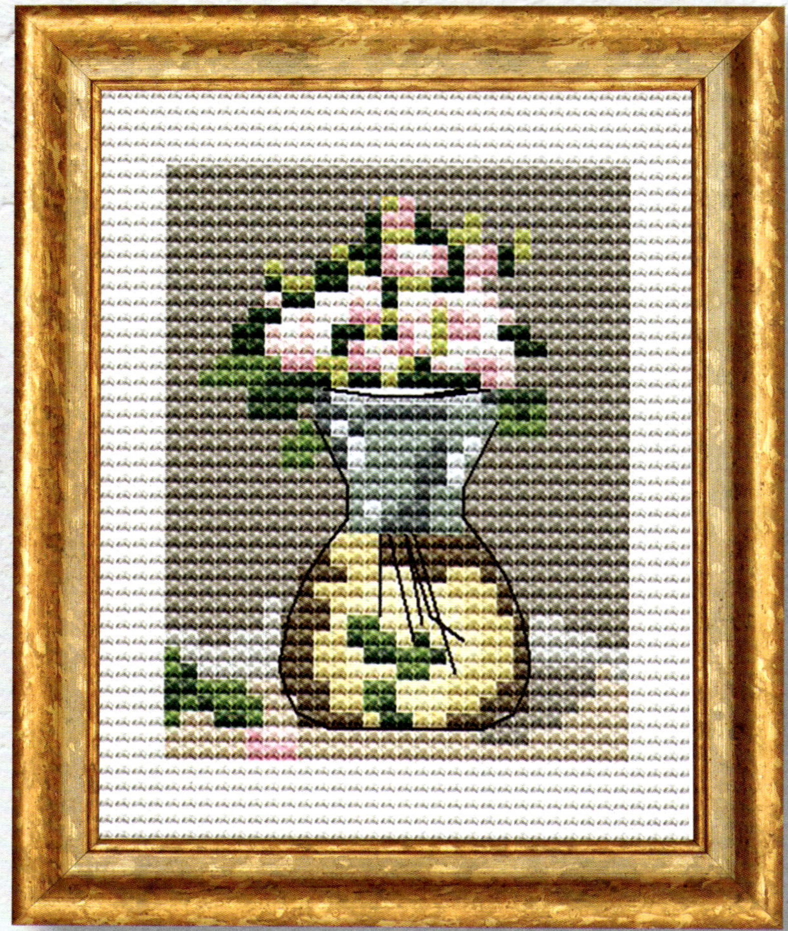

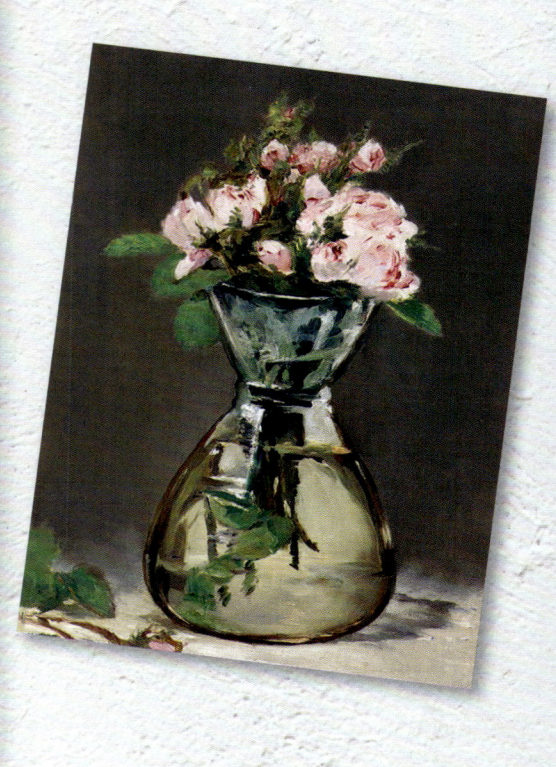

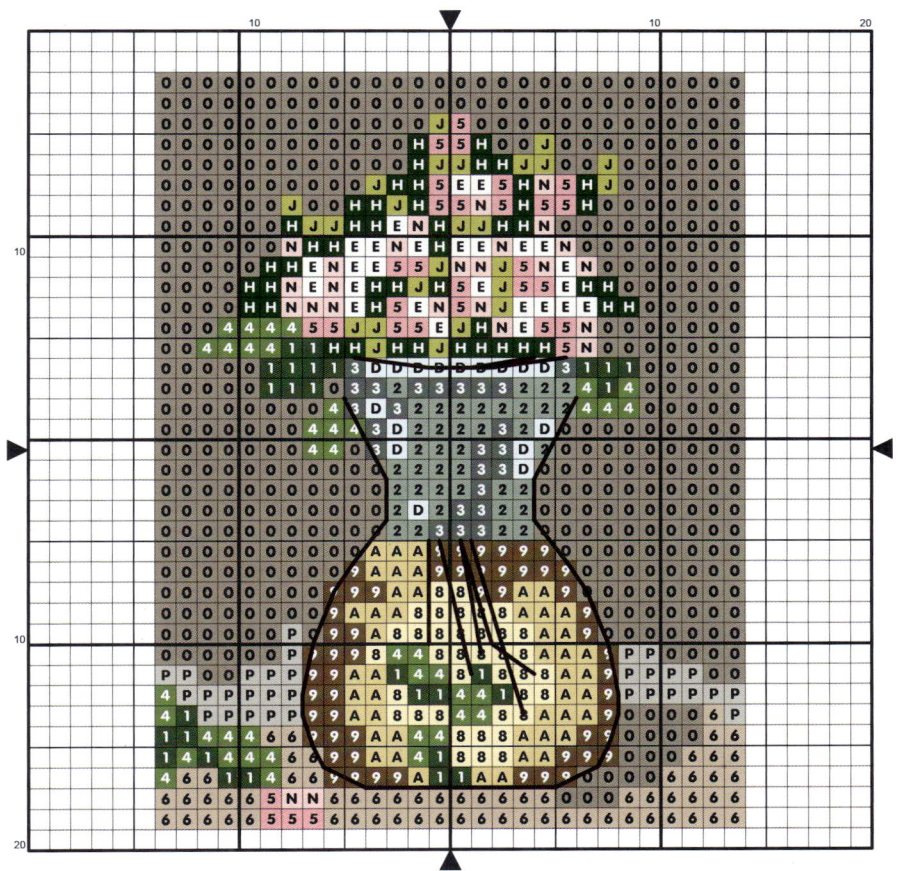

Symbol	Number	Color Name	Symbol	Number	Color Name
0	648	White Pepper	3	926	Grey Green
2	3813	Lichen Green	5	151	Marshmallow
4	989	Fennel	8	3823	Moonshine
6	3033	Ashes	A	677	Metallic Sand
9	640	Grey Cobblestone	E	3865	Edelweiss
D	3756	Cloud Blue	J	472	Green Bud
H	986	Boxwood	P	3072	Thunderous Skies
N	818	Pearlescent Powder Pink		3371	Peppercorn
1	367	Laurel			

Henri Matisse

Daisies

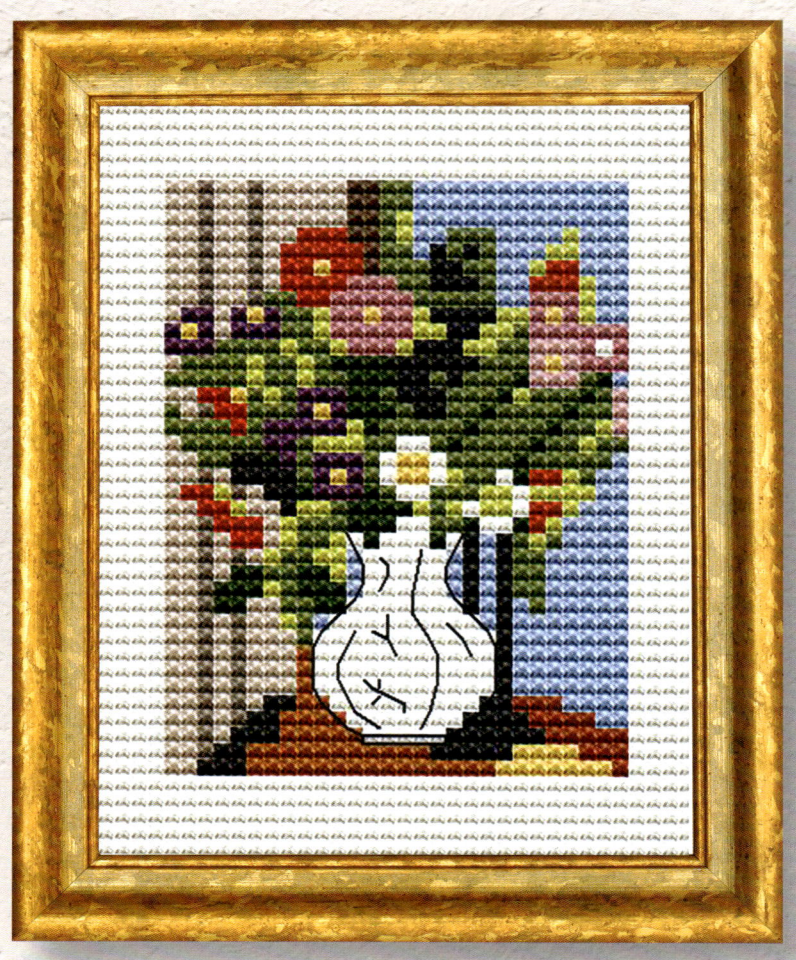
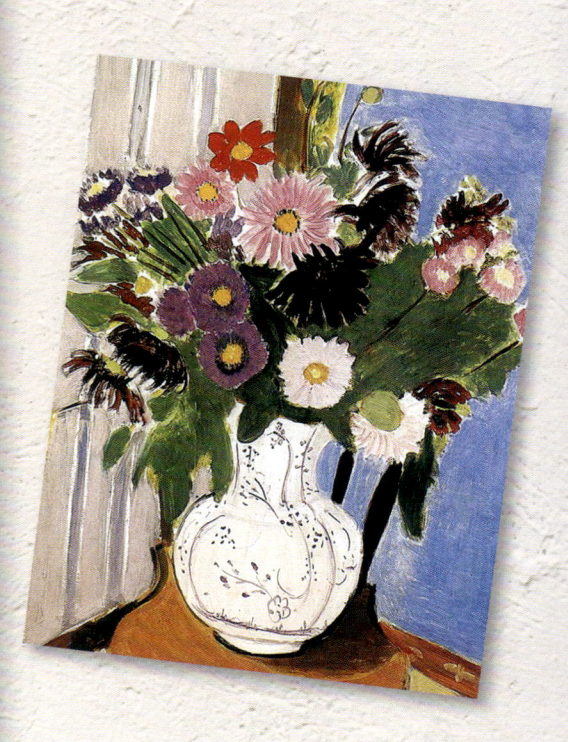

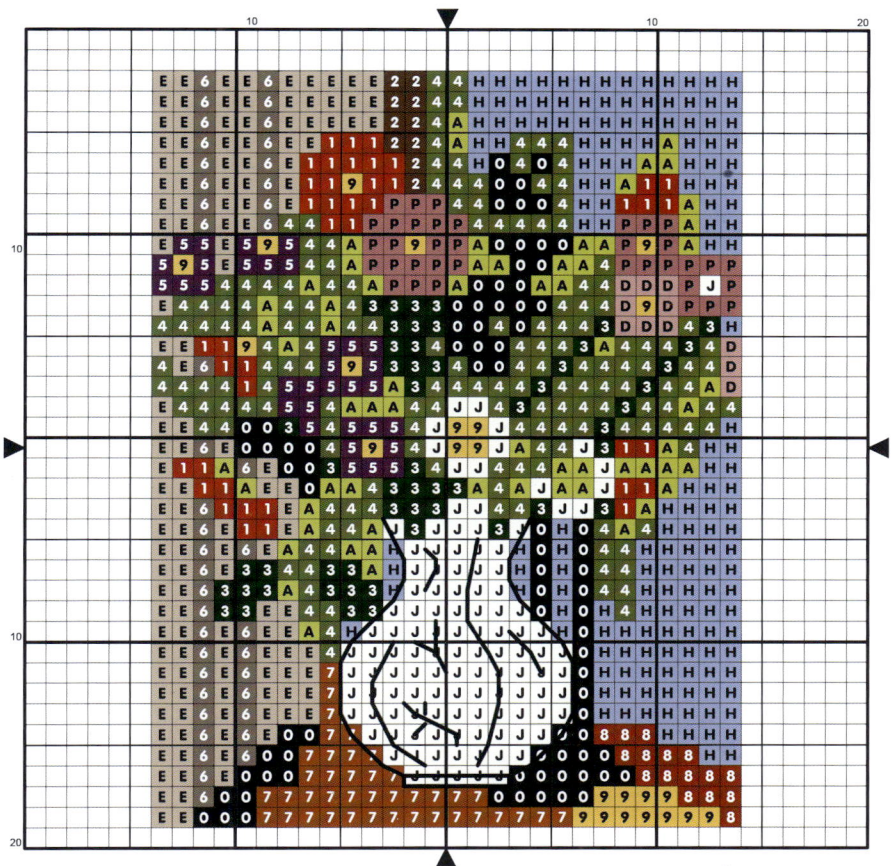

Symbol	Number	Color Name	Symbol	Number	Color Name
O	939	Elderberry Blue	3	890	Black Forest
2	779	Sepia	5	327	Dark Purple
4	3363	Bullfrog	7	301	Metallic Squirrel
6	451	Little Gray	9	676	Savannah
8	919	Terracotta Brown	D	778	Amethyst Haze
A	472	Green Bud	H	3840	Linen Flower Blue
E	453	Dove Gray	P	316	Metallic Heather
J	3865	Edelweiss		939	Elderberry Blue
1	817	Japanese Red			

Henri Matisse

Geranium

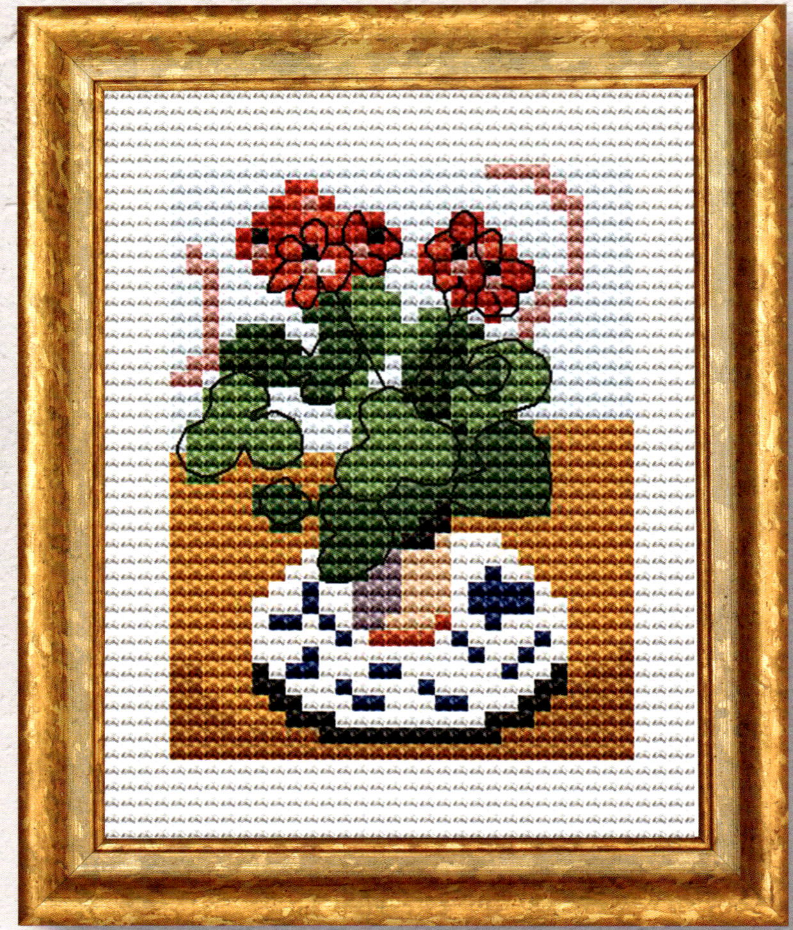

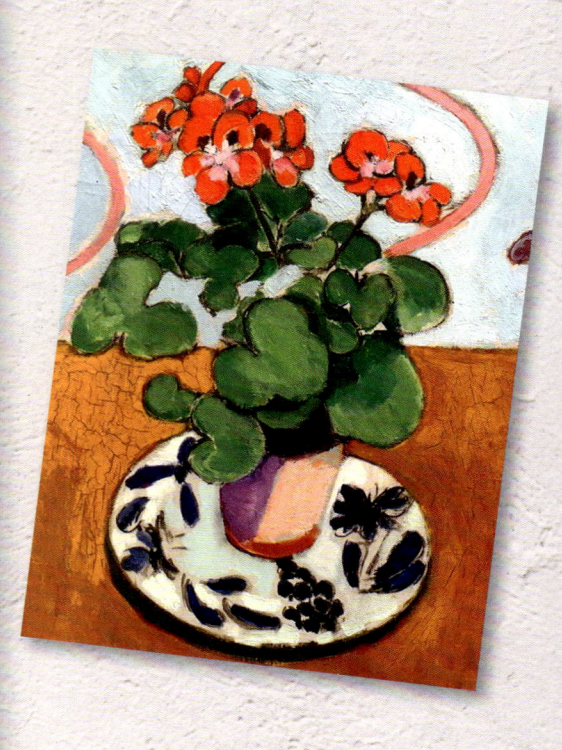

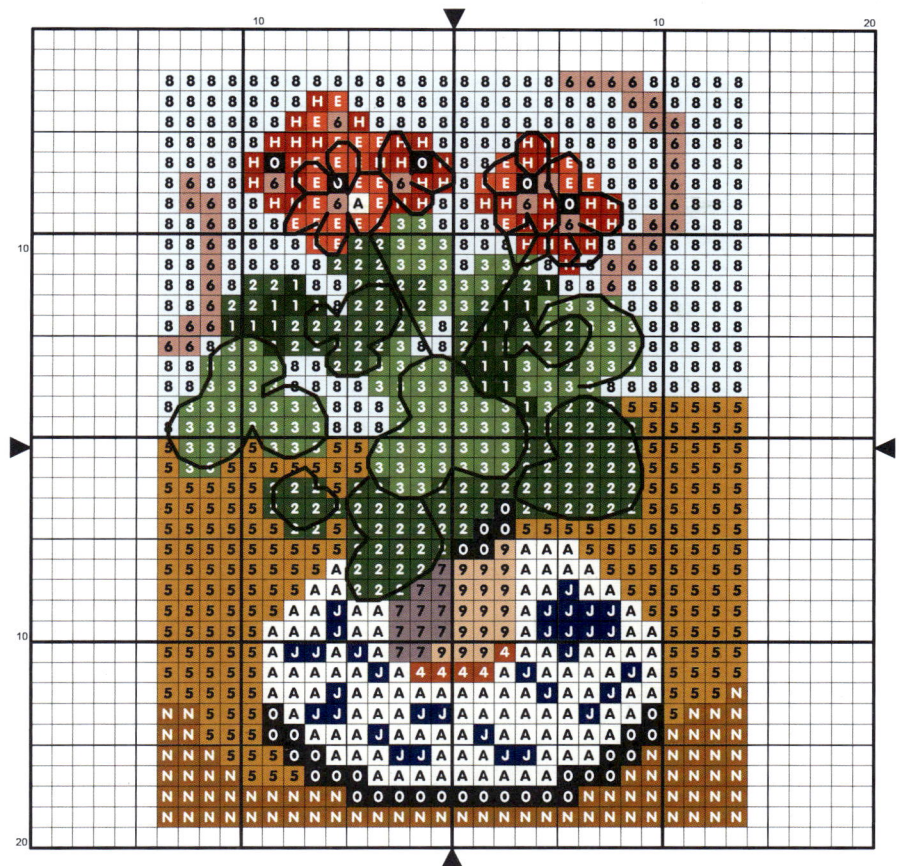

Symbol	Number	Color Name	Symbol	Number	Color Name
O	310	Metallic Black	3	989	Fennel
2	987	Basil	5	783	Old Gold
4	921	Tuscan Ochre	7	3042	Storm Clouds
6	224	Earthworm	9	945	Champagne
8	3756	Cloud Blue	E	351	Coral
A	3865	Edelweiss	J	824	Marine Blue
H	349	Red Pepper	——	310	Metallic Black
N	782	Wicker	——	934	Seaweed
1	3345	Spinach			

Henri Matisse

Vase of Flowers in Front of the Window

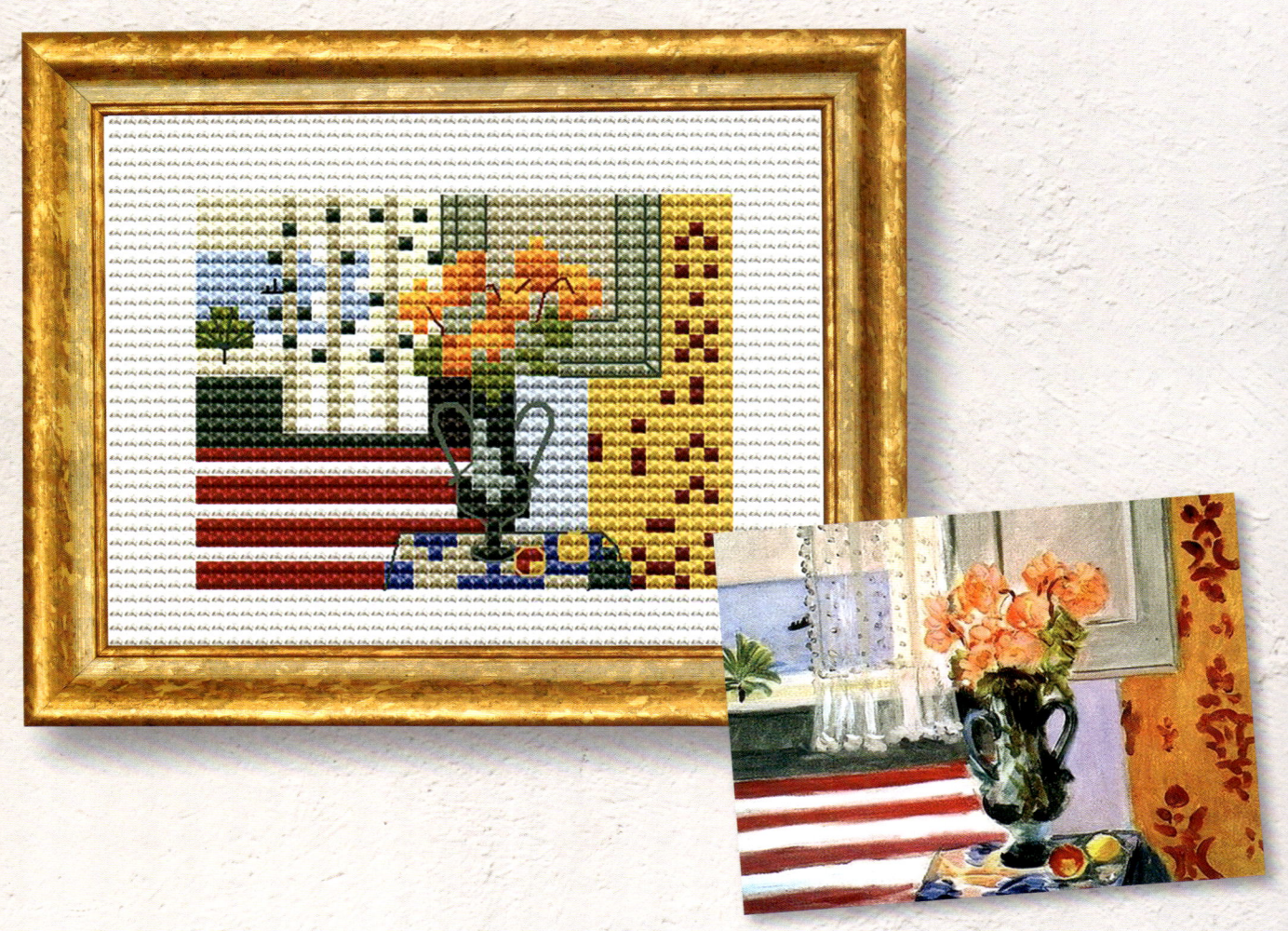

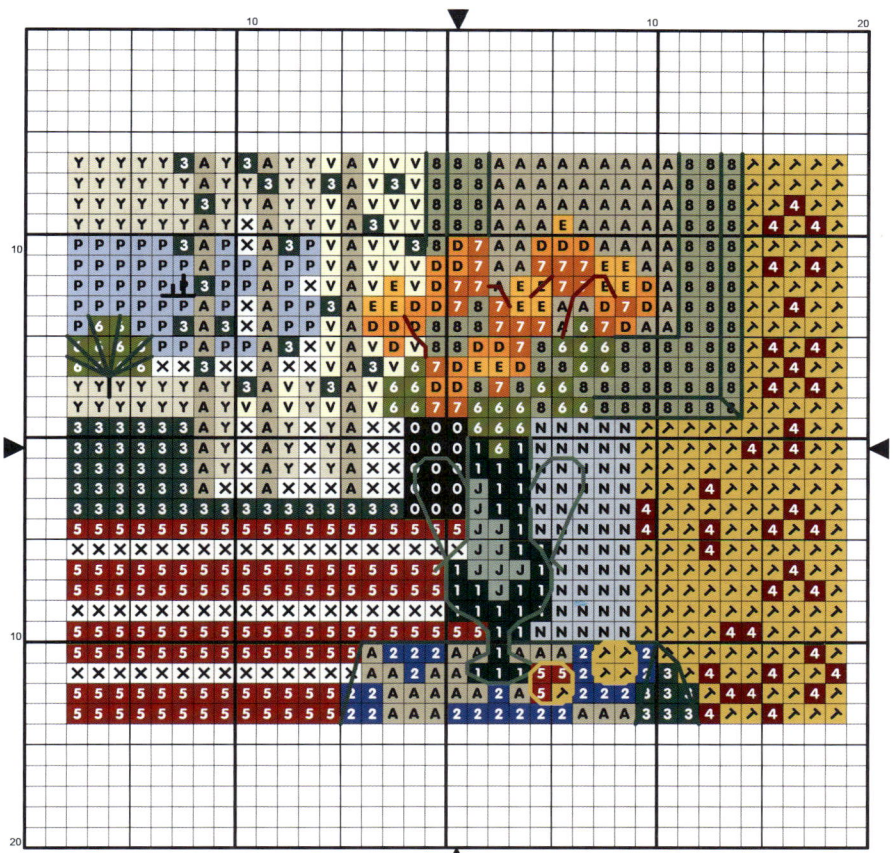

Symbol	Number	Color Name	Symbol	Number	Color Name
O	310	Metallic Black	5	304	Chinese Lacquer
2	798	Cobalt Blue	7	3853	Copper
4	815	Metallic Black Cherry	A	644	Hemp
6	470	Olive Green	E	742	Clementine
8	524	Pebble Green	N	3753	Moonlight Blue
D	741	Mandarin	V	746	Pearlescent Vanilla
J	3813	Lichen Green	X	3865	Edelweiss
P	3325	Arctic Blue	▬	310	Metallic Black
Y	822	Cotton	▬	501	Pond Green
↗	3821	Metallic Mango	▬	815	Metallic Black Cherry
1	500	Ivy	▬	502	Almond Leaf
3	501	Pond Green	▬	3821	Metallic Mango

57

Luis Egidio Meléndez

Still Life with Watermelons and Apples

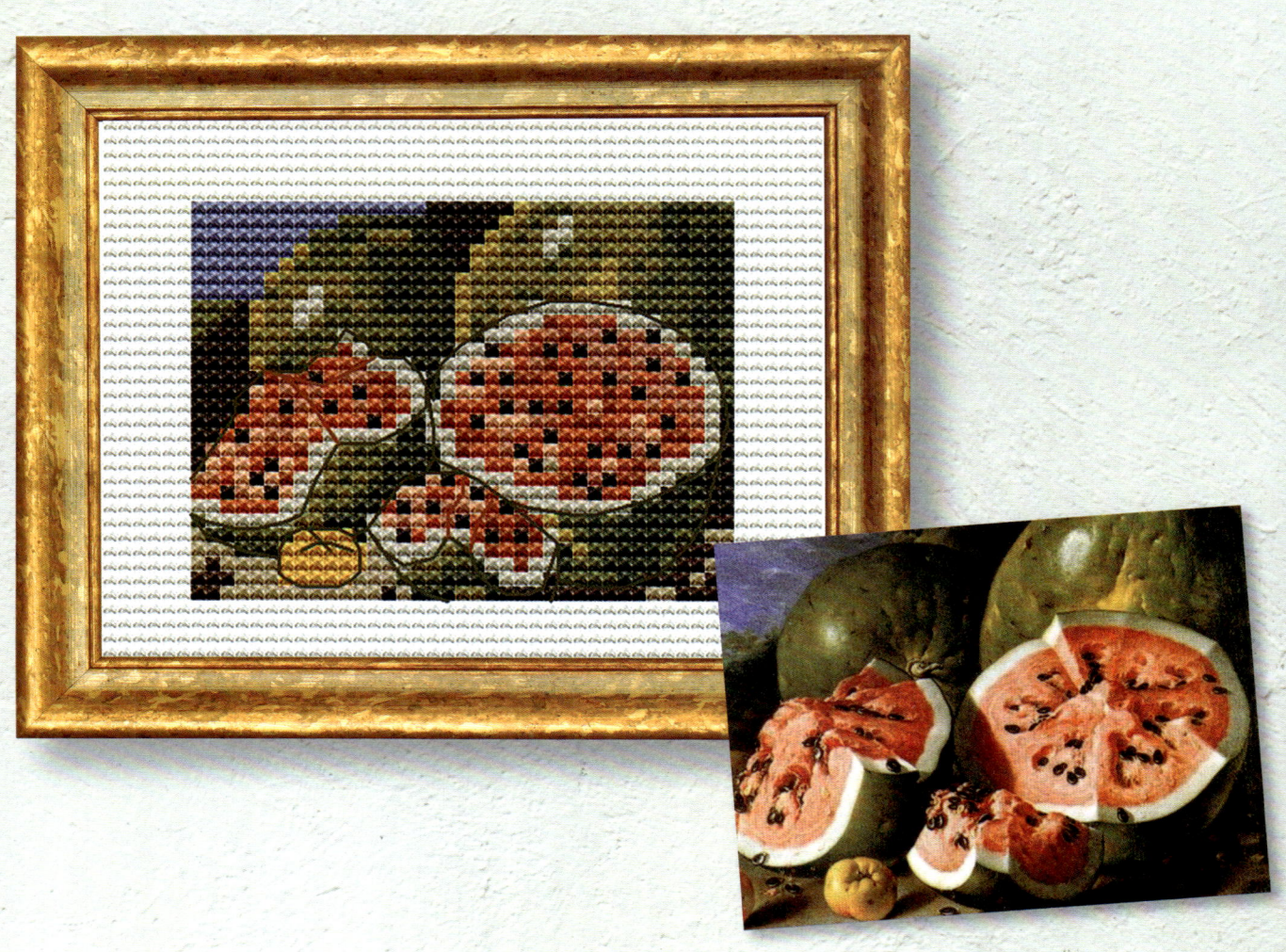

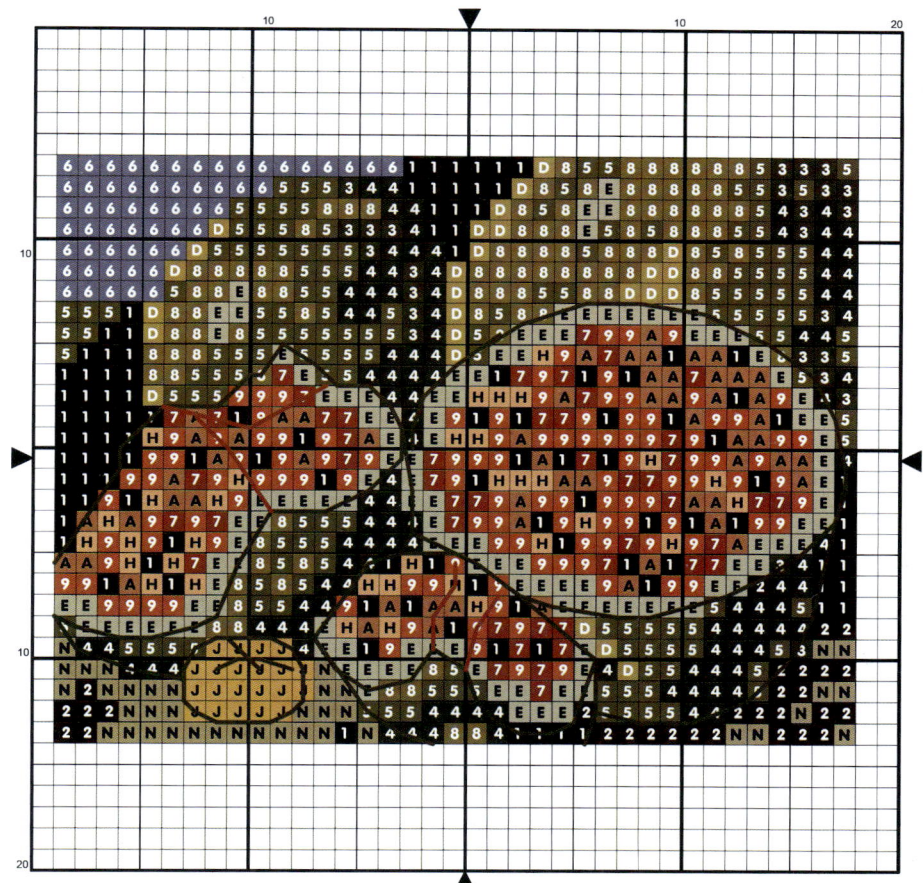

Symbol	Number	Color Name	Symbol	Number	Color Name
1	3371	Peppercorn	4	935	Undergrowth
3	936	Oak Moss	6	160	Stormy Blue
5	3011	Deep Olive	8	370	Herbes de Provence
7	301	Metallic Squirrel	A	3064	Fallow
9	3776	Nut Brittle	E	3024	Silver Linings
D	833	Brass	J	3820	Sunshine
H	3771	Pink Sand	—	936	Oak Moss
N	3782	Ginger	—	301	Metallic Squirrel
2	938	Clove			

Claude Monet

Bouquet of Sunflowers

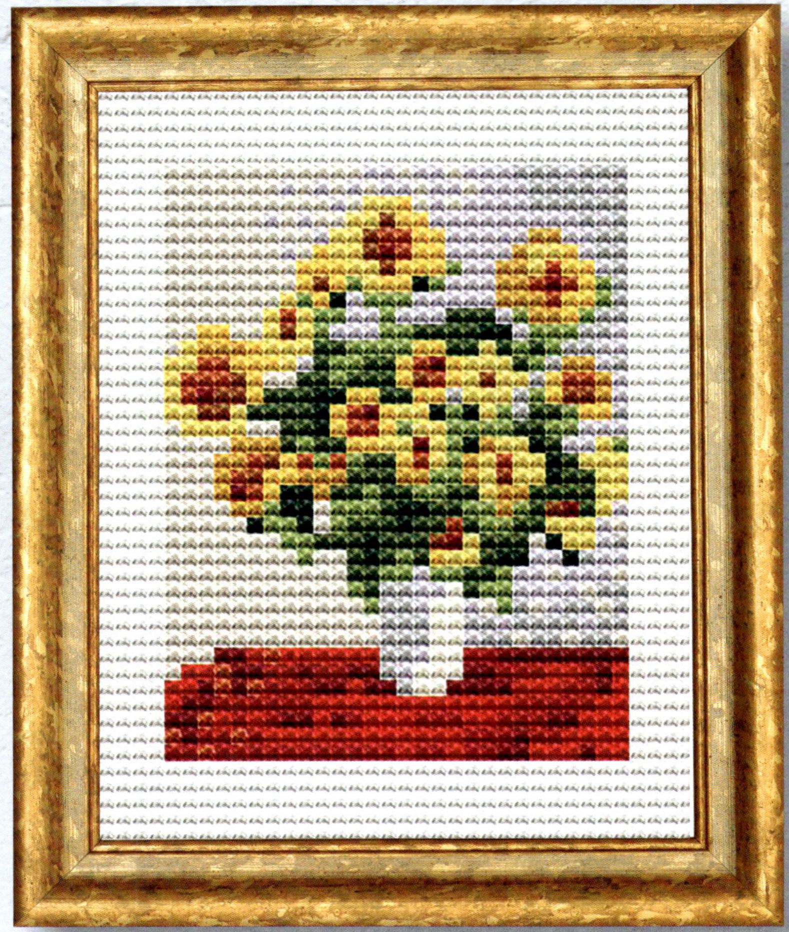

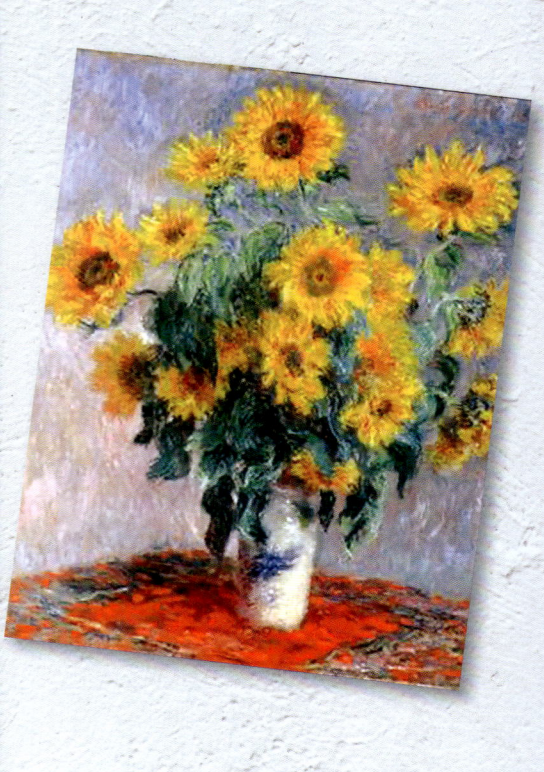

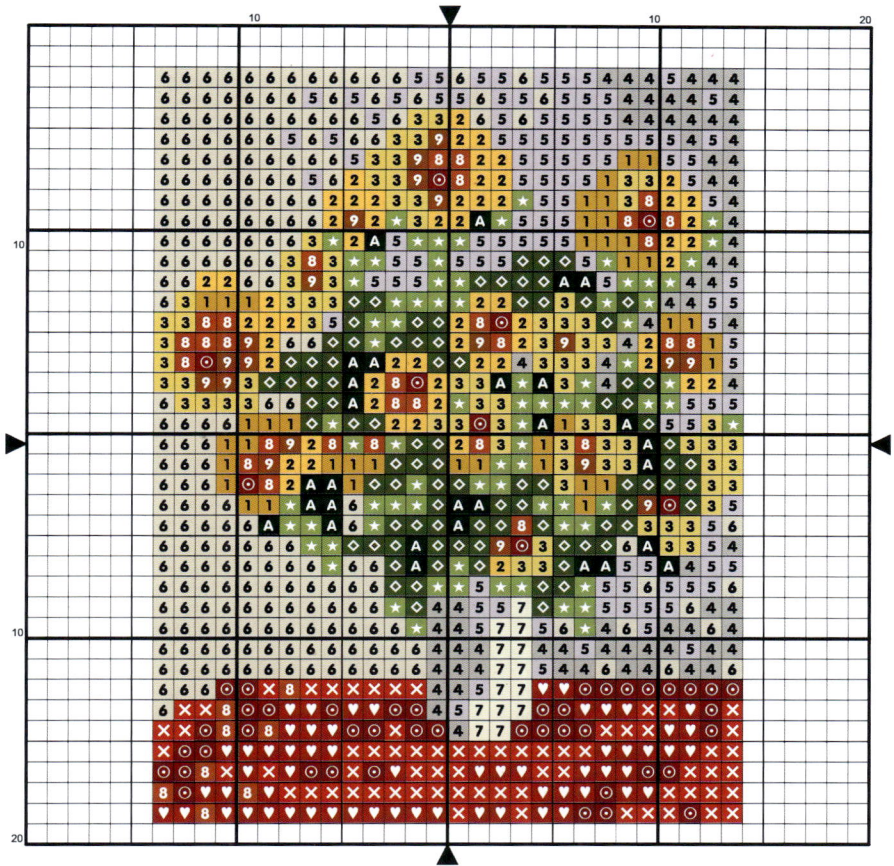

Symbol	Number	Color Name	Symbol	Number	Color Name
◇	3346	Artichoke	✖	666	Scarlet
♥	321	Metallic Carmine Red	⊙	498	Red Kiss
★	471	Tarragon	1	3820	Sunshine
2	725	Buttercup	3	3822	Corn Husk
4	02	Mist	5	25	Cornflower White
6	3866	Garlic White	7	712	Cream
8	921	Tuscan Ochre	9	3826	Fox
A	890	Black Forest			

Claude Monet

Christmas Roses

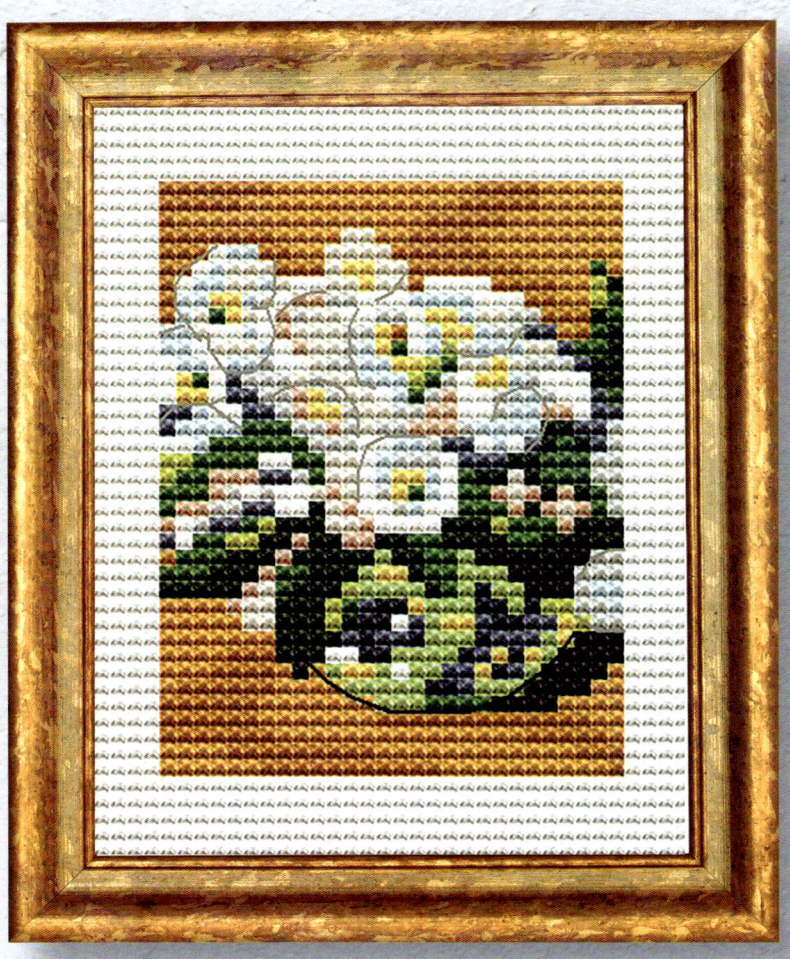
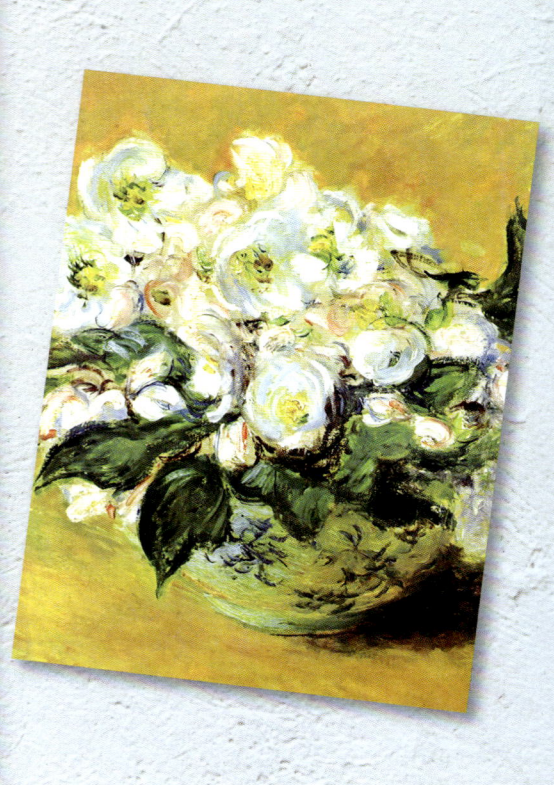

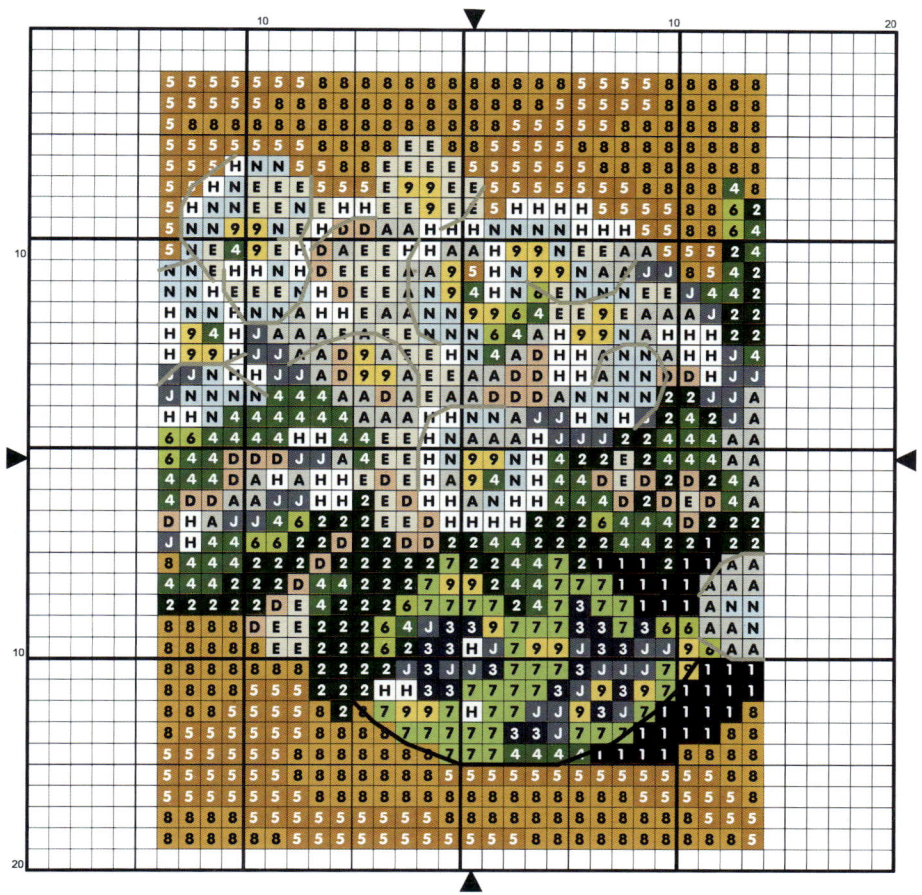

Symbol	Number	Color Name	Symbol	Number	Color Name
1	939	Elderberry Blue	4	905	Budgie Green
3	3750	Dark Petrol Blue	6	3819	Aurous Green
5	3852	Metallic Glitz	8	3820	Sunshine
7	3348	Scallion	A	3072	Thunderous Skies
9	3822	Corn Husk	E	3866	Garlic White
D	950	Beige	J	931	Blue Grey
H	3865	Edelweiss	—	939	Elderberry Blue
N	775	Blue Summer Rain	—	648	White Pepper
2	890	Black Forest			

Claude Monet

Chrysanthemums

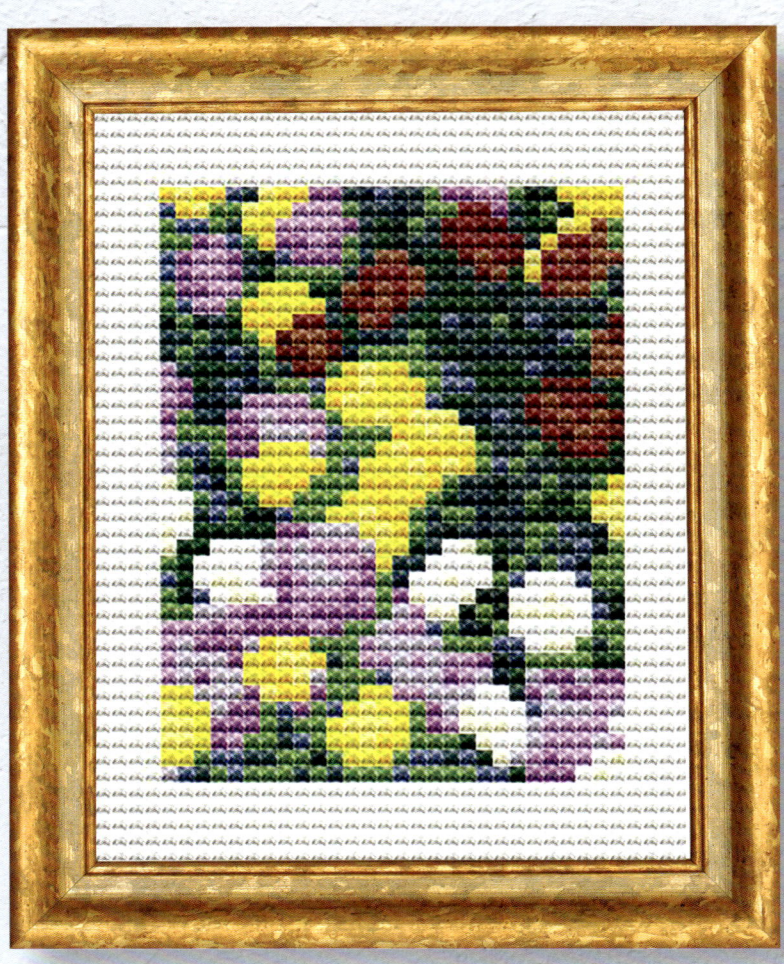
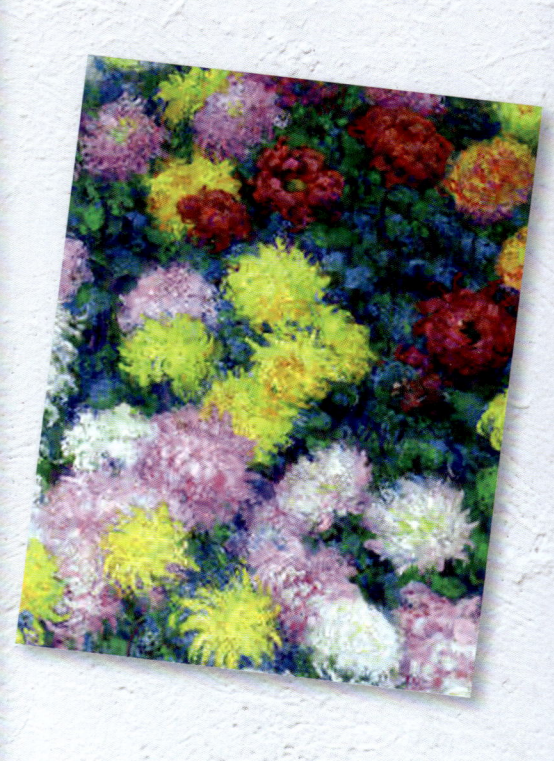

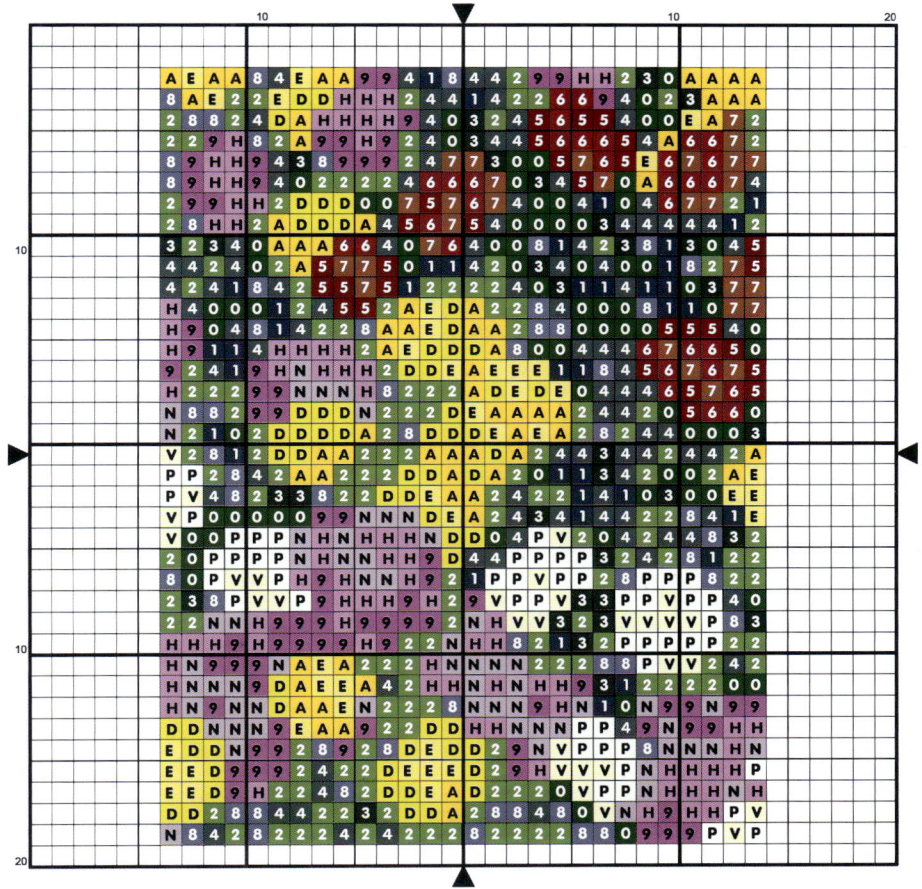

Symbol	Number	Color Name	Symbol	Number	Color Name
O	986	Boxwood	1	930	Slate Grey
2	989	Fennel	3	500	Ivy
4	3768	Storm	5	221	Mars Red
6	3721	Pink Earth	7	3772	Glazed Chestnut
8	160	Stormy Blue	9	209	Lilac
A	973	Daffodil	D	307	Lemon
E	727	Primrose	H	210	Parma Violet
N	26	Lavender White	P	3865	Edelweiss
V	746	Pearlescent Vanilla			

Claude Monet

Nasturtiums in a Blue Vase

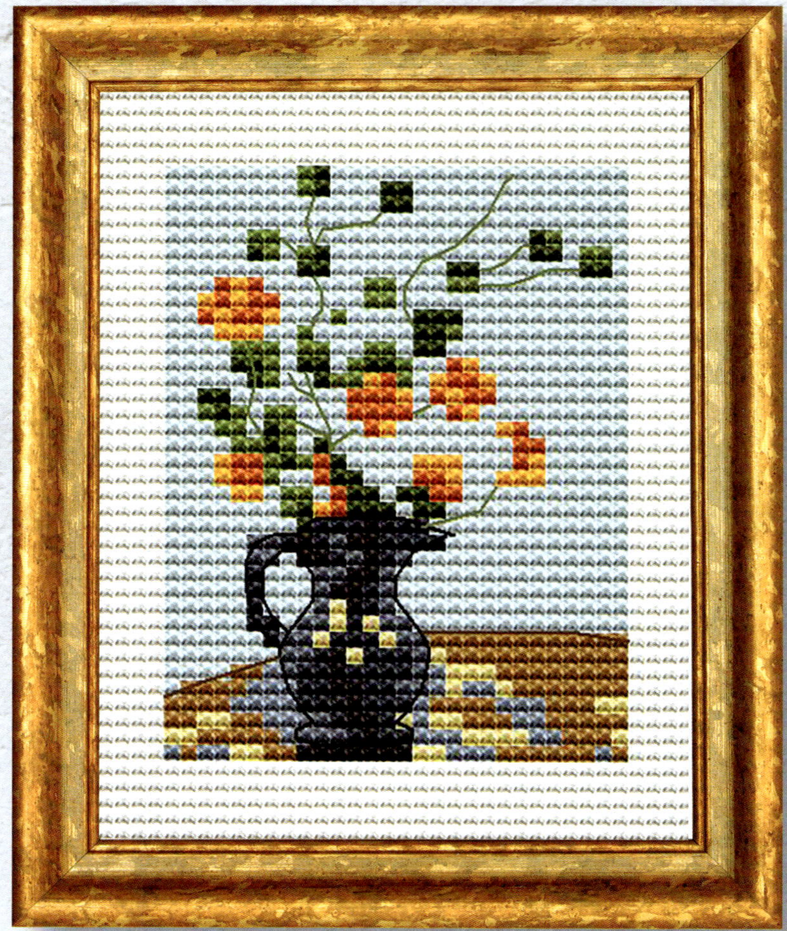

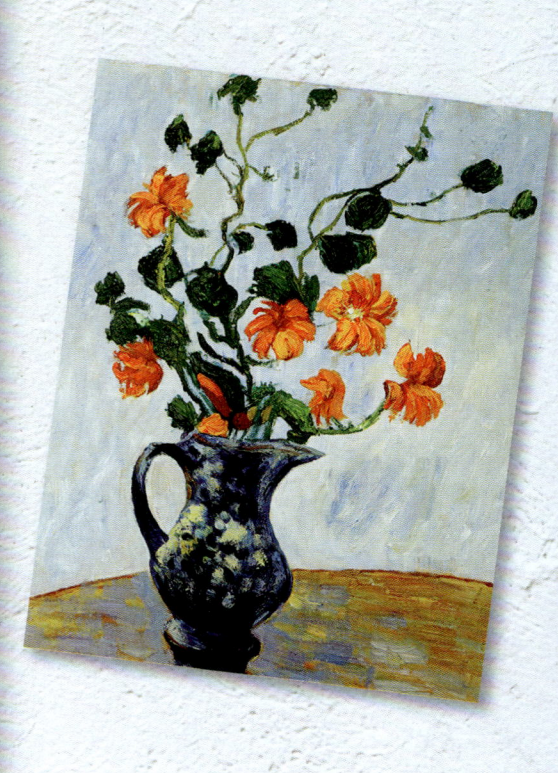

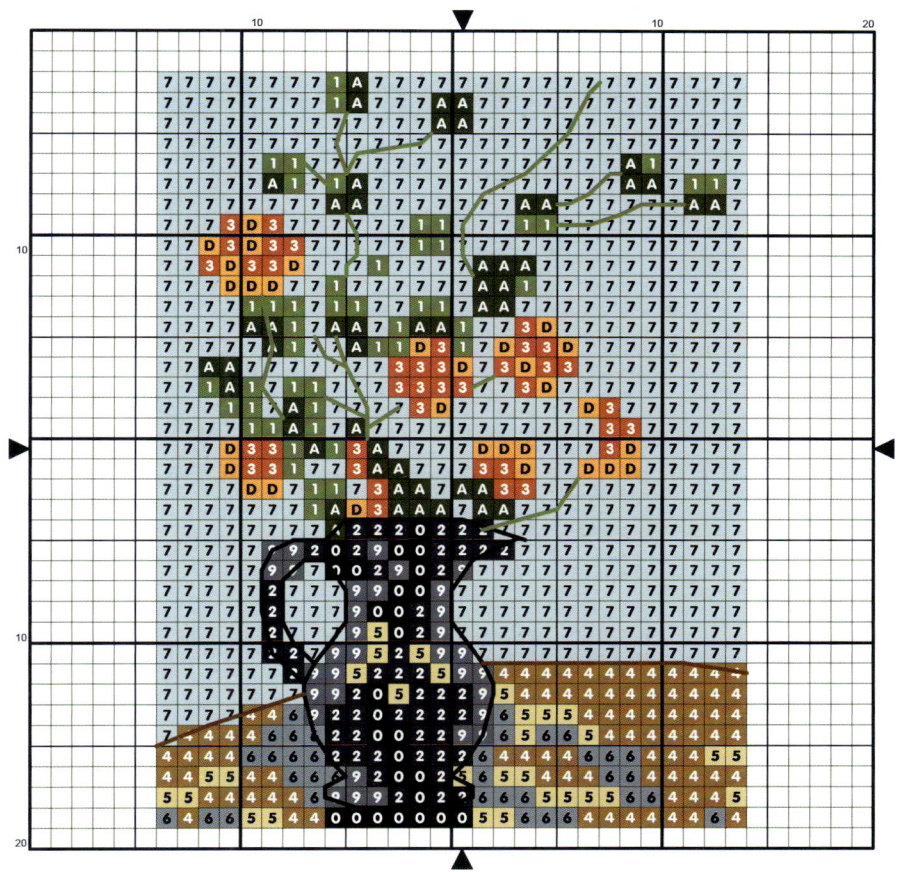

Symbol	Number	Color Name	Symbol	Number	Color Name
0	939	Elderberry Blue	3	3853	Copper
2	3750	Dark Petrol Blue	5	677	Metallic Sand
4	3828	Oak	7	775	Blue Summer Rain
6	932	Blue Gull	A	3345	Spinach
9	931	Blue Grey	—	939	Elderberry Blue
D	742	Clementine	—	3347	Asparagus
1	3347	Asparagus	—	869	Coffee

Claude Monet

Three Pots of Tulips

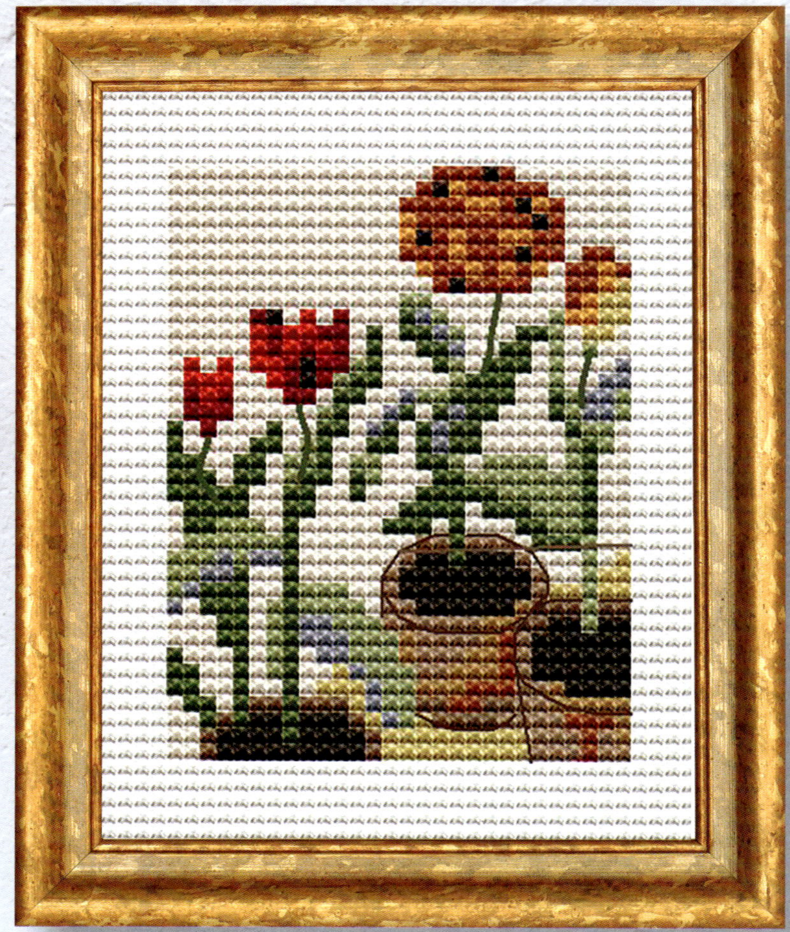

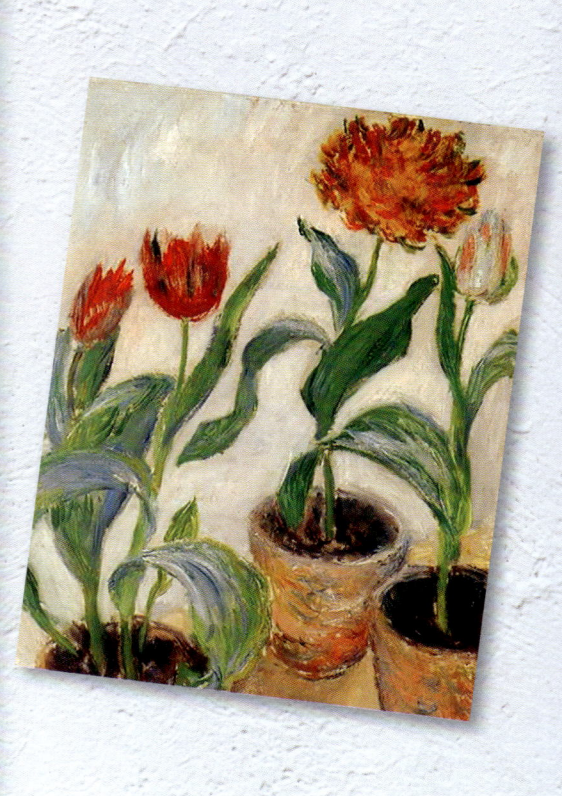

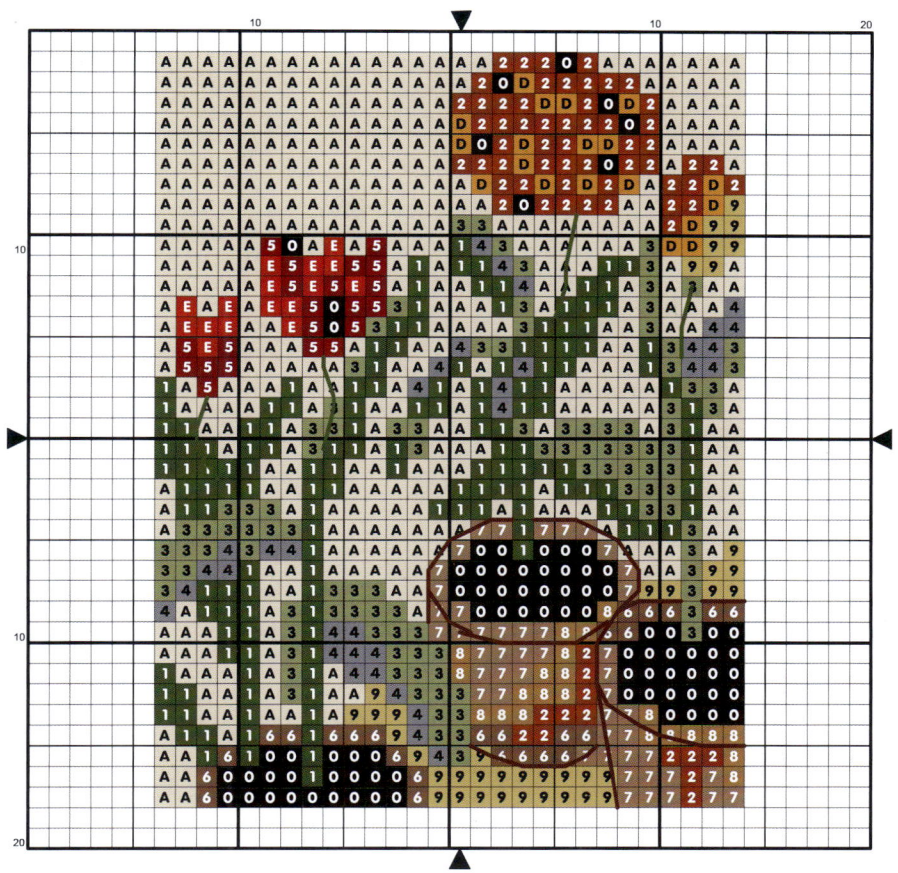

Symbol	Number	Color Name	Symbol	Number	Color Name
O	3371	Peppercorn	3	3053	Avocado
2	301	Metallic Squirrel	5	498	Red Kiss
4	318	Granite Grey	7	841	Suede
6	840	Country Mouse	9	3046	Biscuit
8	3828	Oak	D	783	Old Gold
A	3866	Garlic White	——	3346	Artichoke
E	349	Red Pepper	——	801	Mink
1	3346	Artichoke			

Claude Monet

Water Lilies

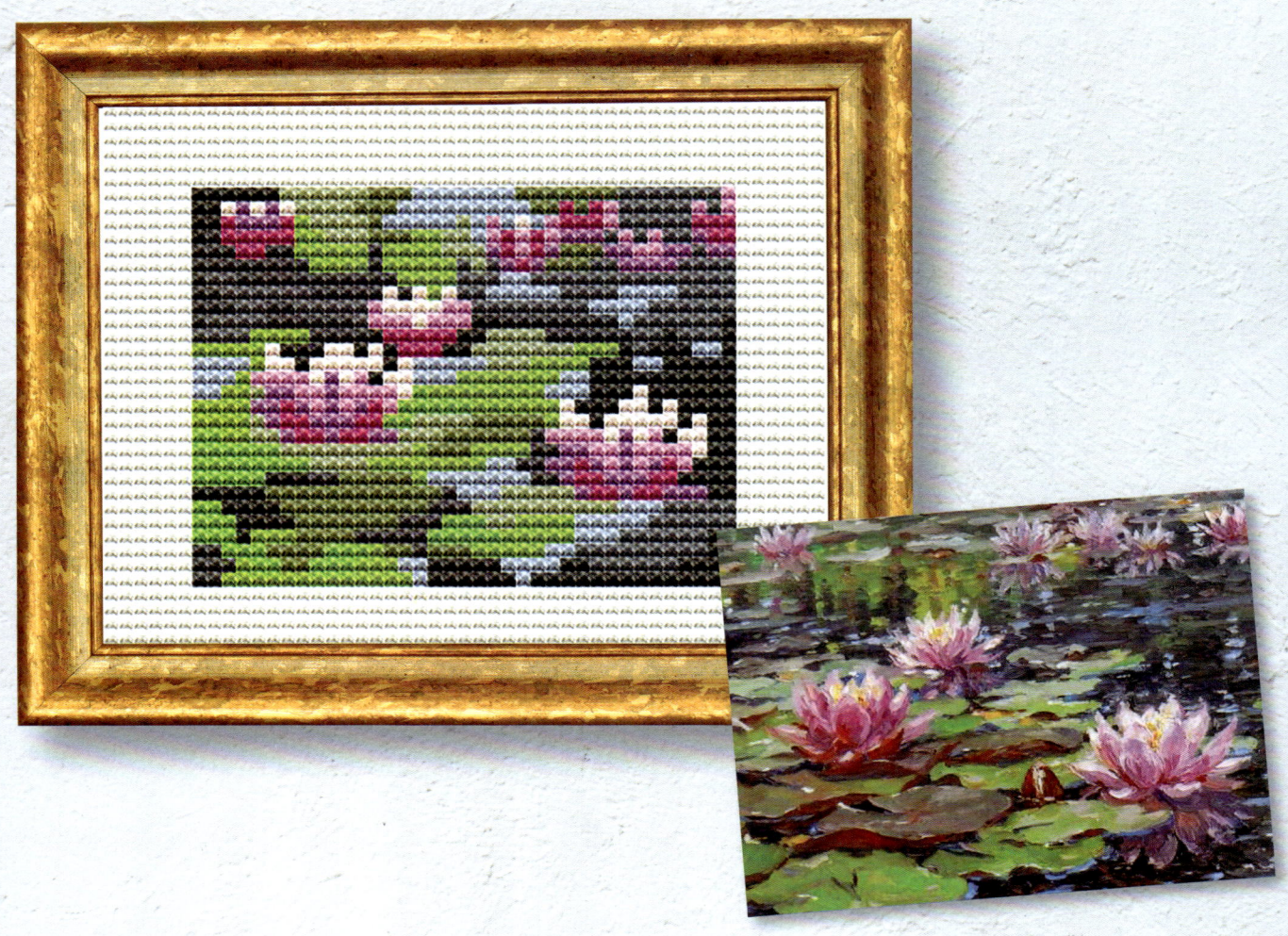

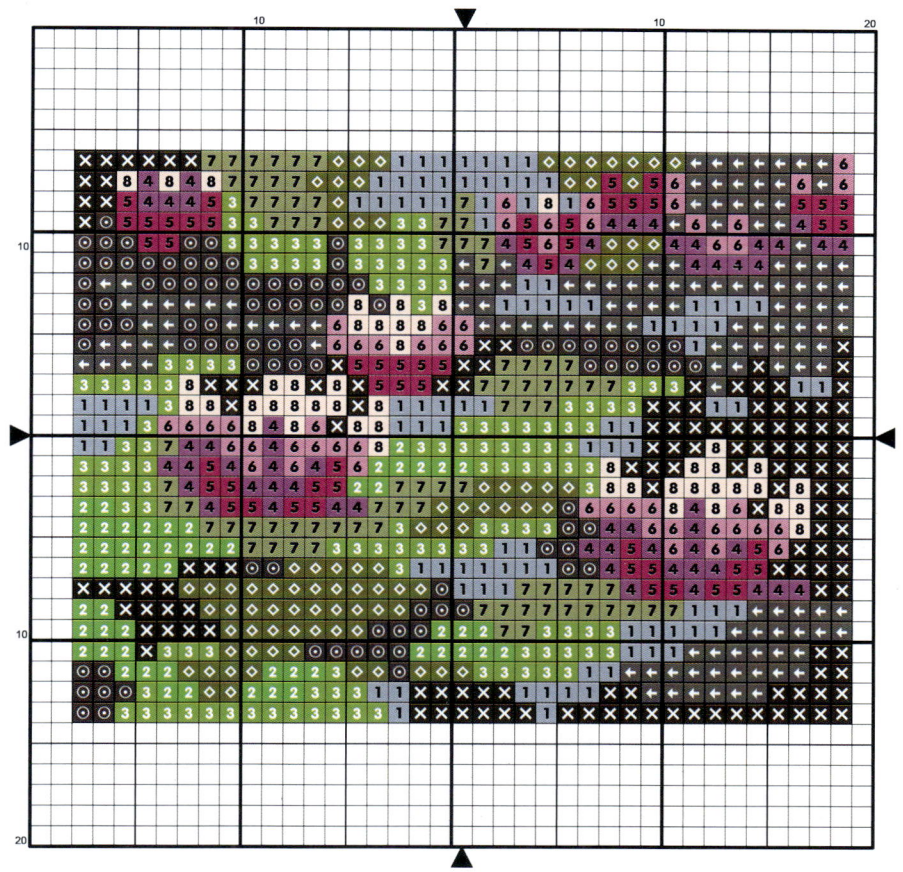

Symbol	Number	Color Name	Symbol	Number	Color Name
❌	413	Iron	◉	317	Metallic Steel
←	414	Lead	◇	3052	Silver Green
1	157	Heliotrope	2	704	Lime
3	907	Granny Smith	4	209	Lilac
5	3607	Hibiscus	6	3609	Lotus Blossom
7	524	Pebble Green	8	819	Layette

Odilon Redon

Poppies and Daisies

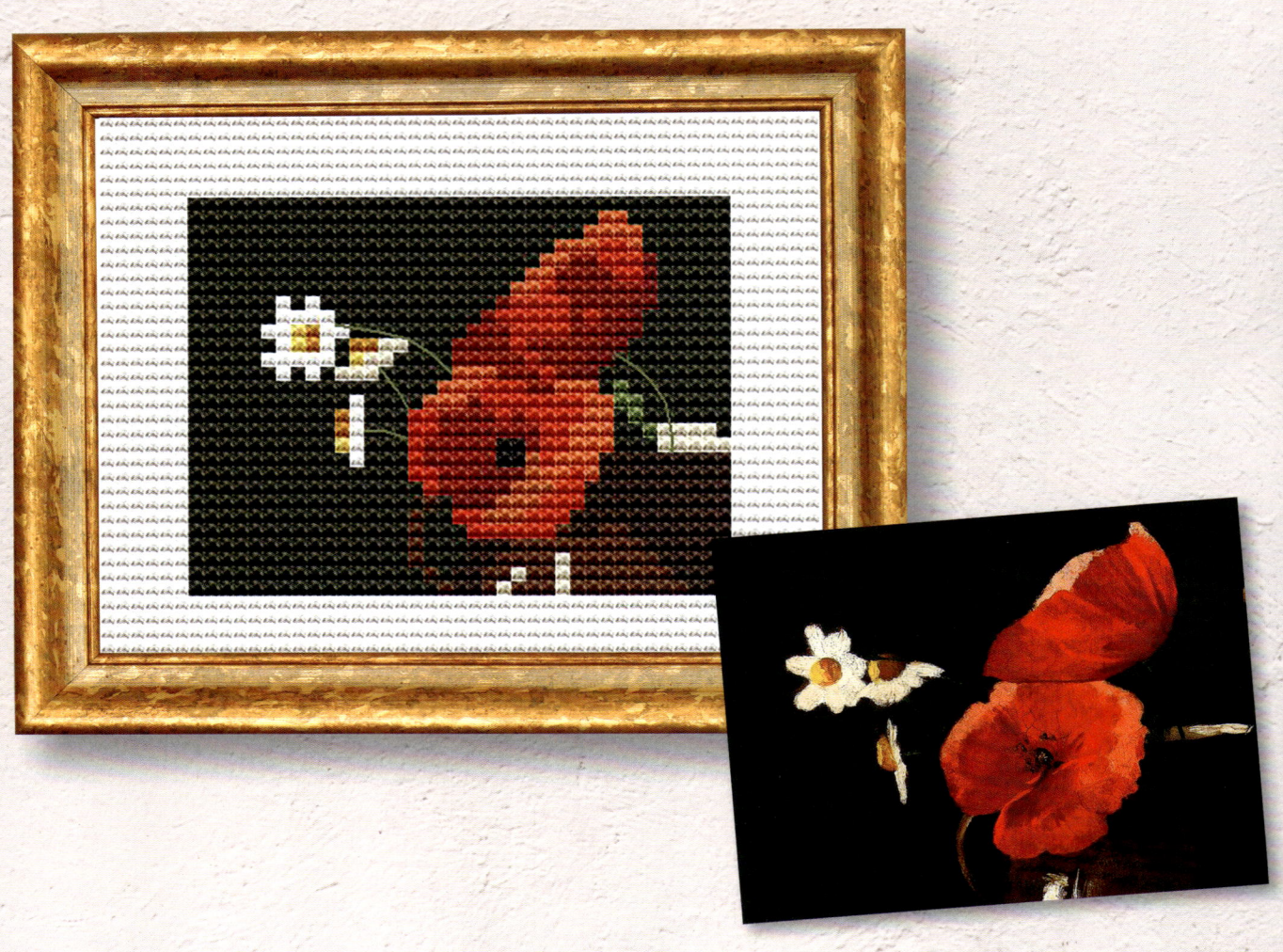

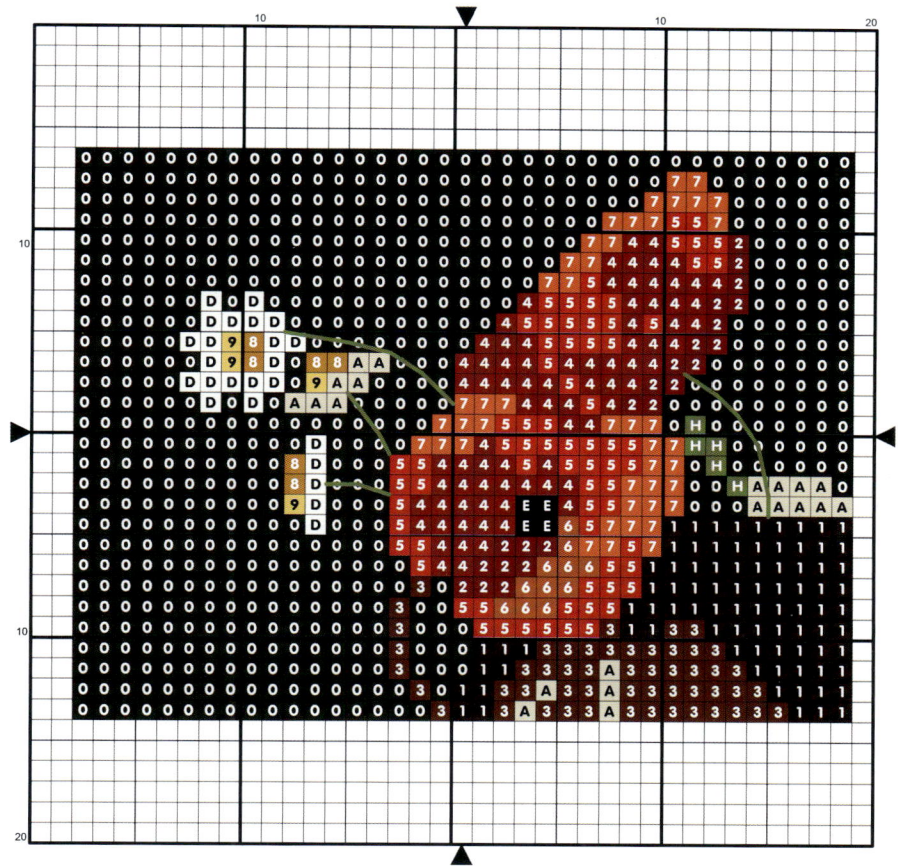

Symbol	Number	Color Name	Symbol	Number	Color Name
0	934	Seaweed	3	433	Chocolate
2	3777	Red Leather	5	900	Blood Orange
4	919	Terracotta Brown	7	922	Terracotta
6	3776	Nut Brittle	9	3822	Corn Husk
8	3852	Metallic Glitz	D	3865	Edelweiss
A	822	Cotton	H	3347	Asparagus
E	310	Metallic Black		3347	Asparagus
1	938	Clove			

Pierre-Joseph Redouté

Vase of Flowers

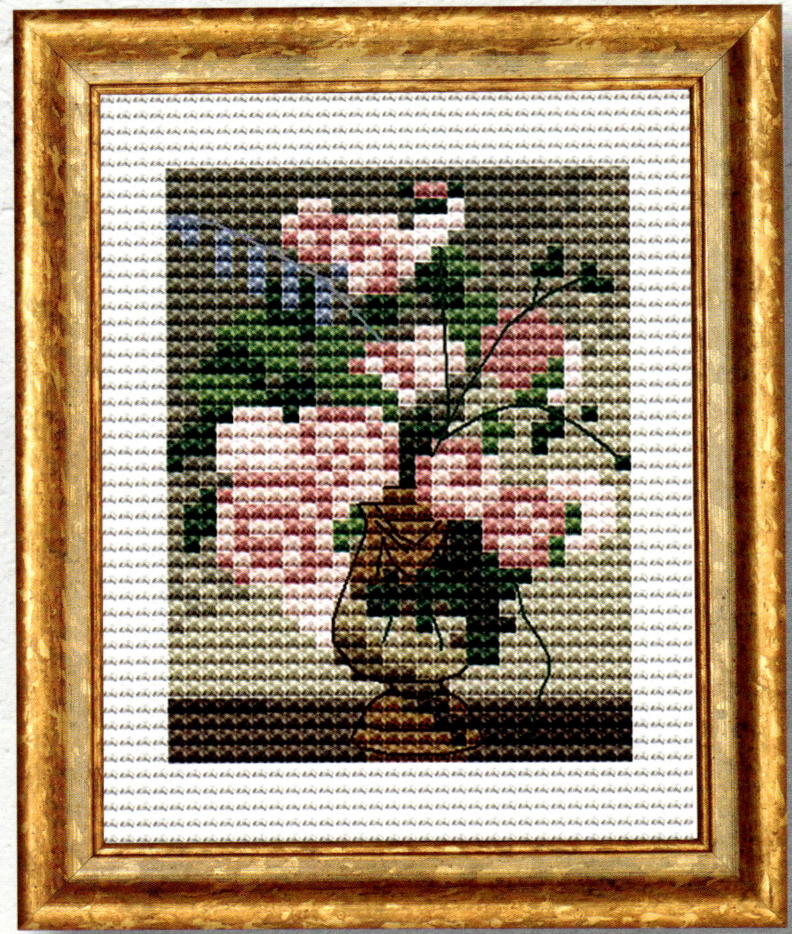

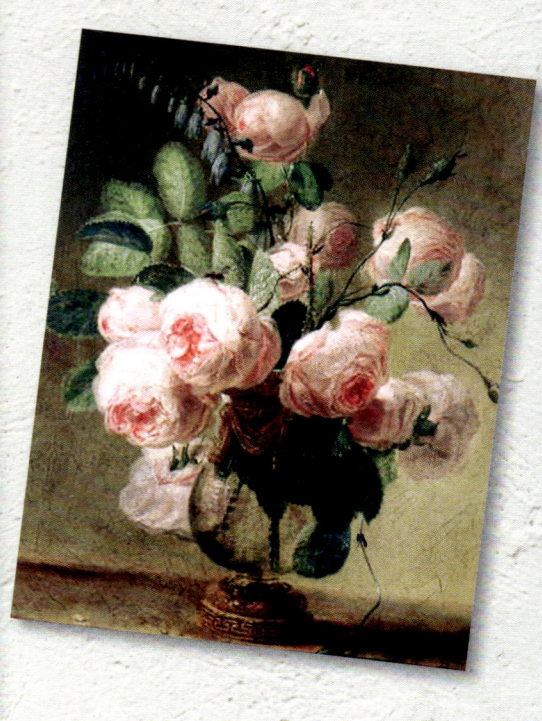

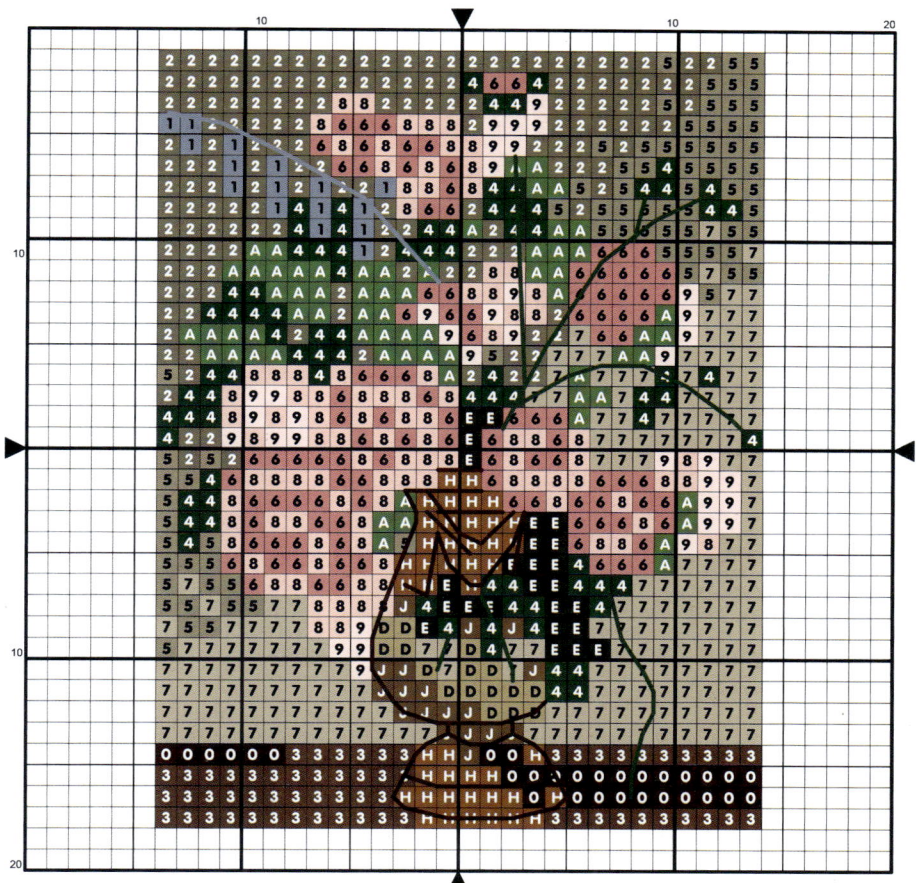

Symbol	Number	Color Name	Symbol	Number	Color Name
0	938	Clove	3	3790	Tree Bark
2	3022	Rhino	5	3023	Elephant
4	986	Boxwood	7	644	Hemp
6	152	Old Pink	9	819	Layette
8	225	Cherry Blossom	D	613	Twine
A	988	Verbena Stem	H	420	Hazelnut
E	934	Seaweed	———	938	Clove
J	611	Umber	———	932	Blue Gull
1	932	Blue Gull	———	986	Boxwood

Pierre-Auguste Renoir

Anemones

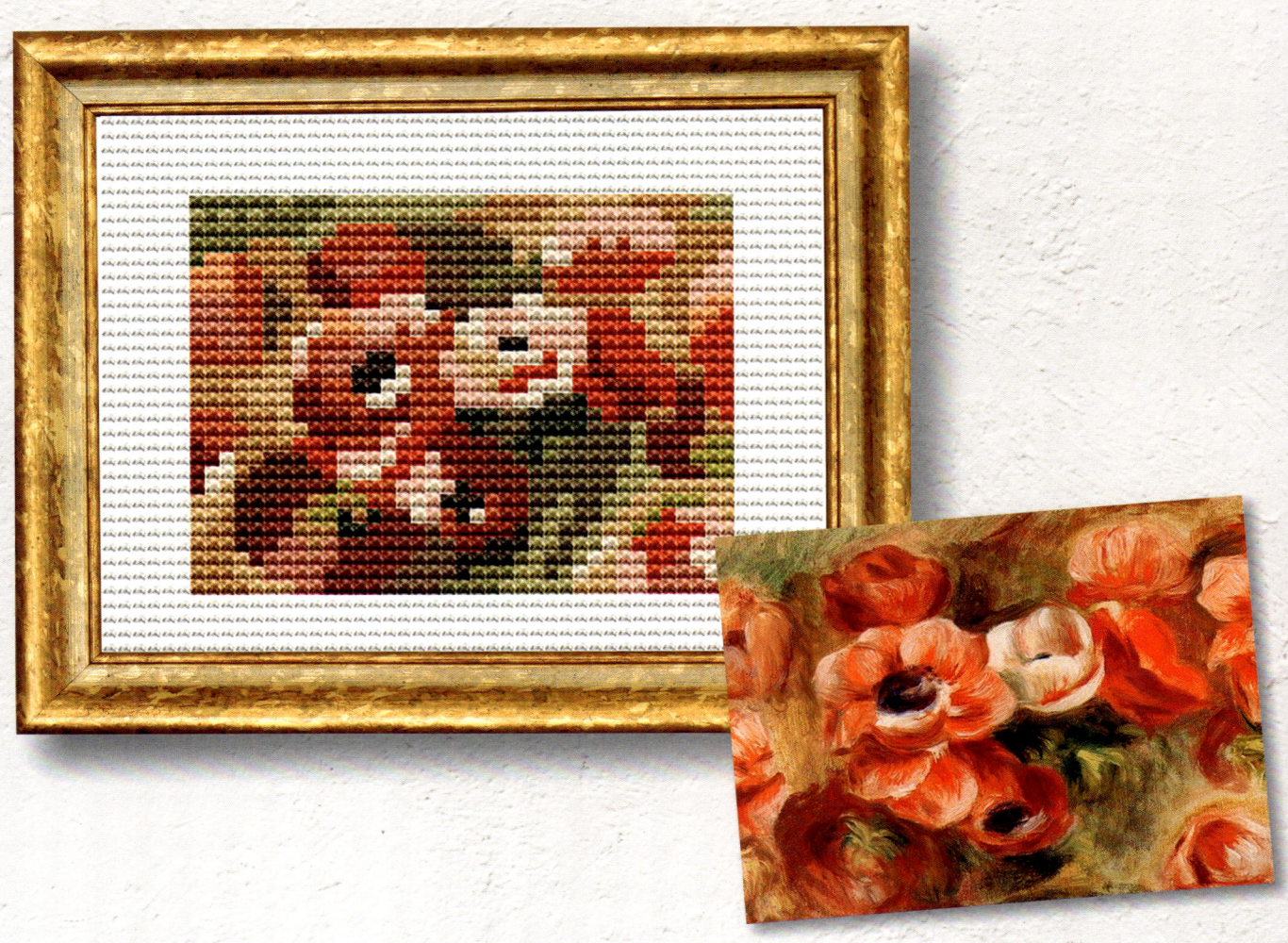

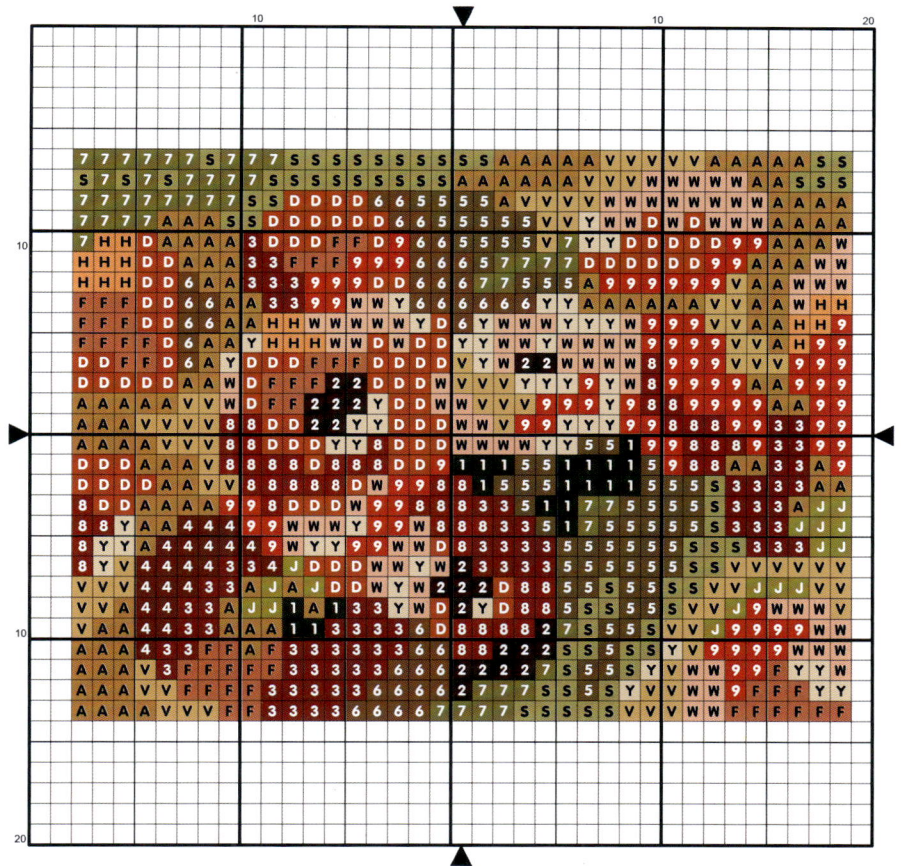

Symbol	Number	Color Name	Symbol	Number	Color Name
1	935	Undergrowth	2	838	Dark Wood
3	355	Red Brown	4	400	Conker
5	611	Umber	6	3862	Lama
7	3012	Dried Moss	8	919	Terracotta Brown
9	900	Blood Orange	A	436	Metallic Teddy
D	921	Tuscan Ochre	F	3778	Rose Gold
H	402	Pottery	J	733	Golden Green
S	372	Cardamon Green	V	437	Camel
W	3779	Burnished Pink	Y	543	Shell

Pierre-Auguste Renoir

Bouquet of Roses

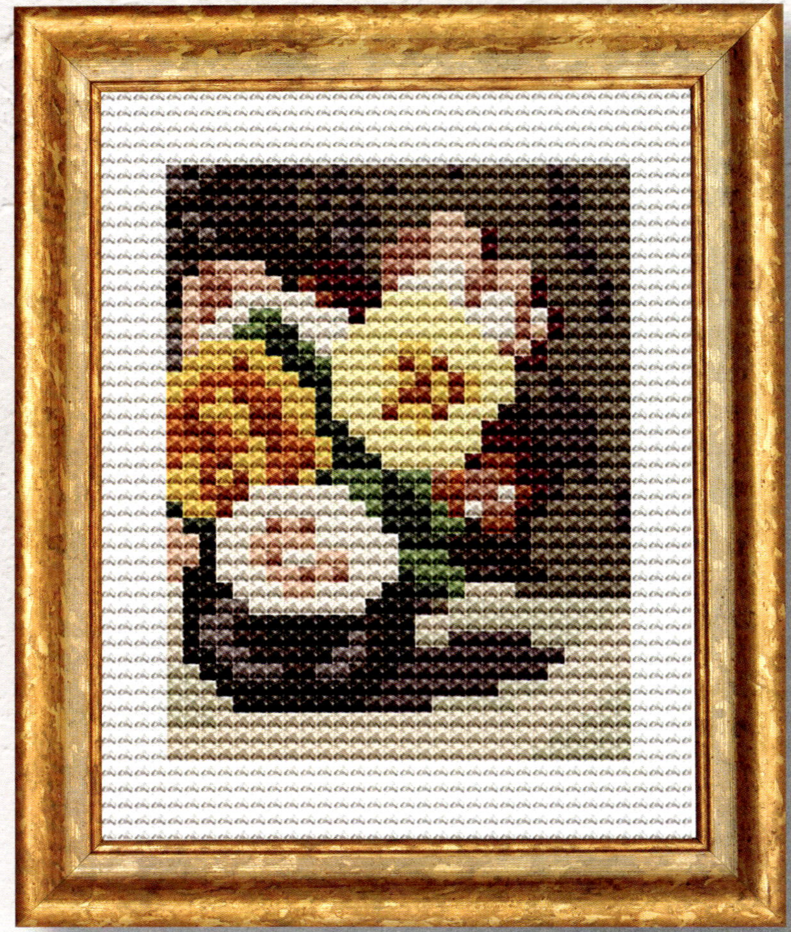

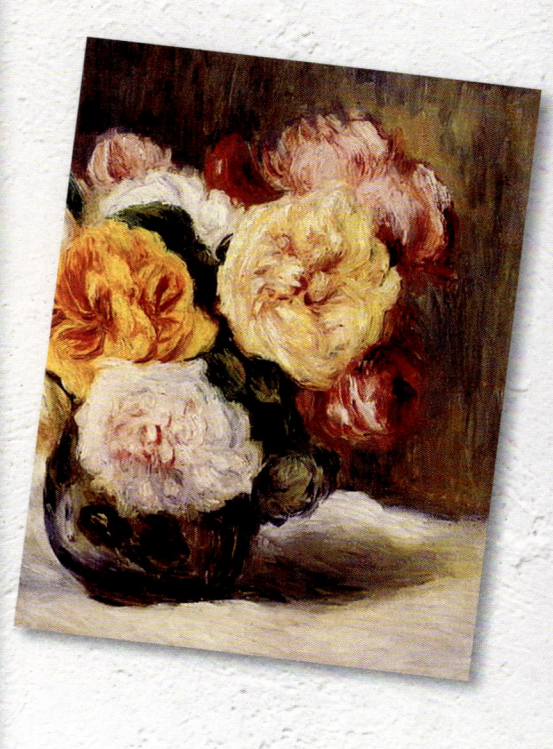

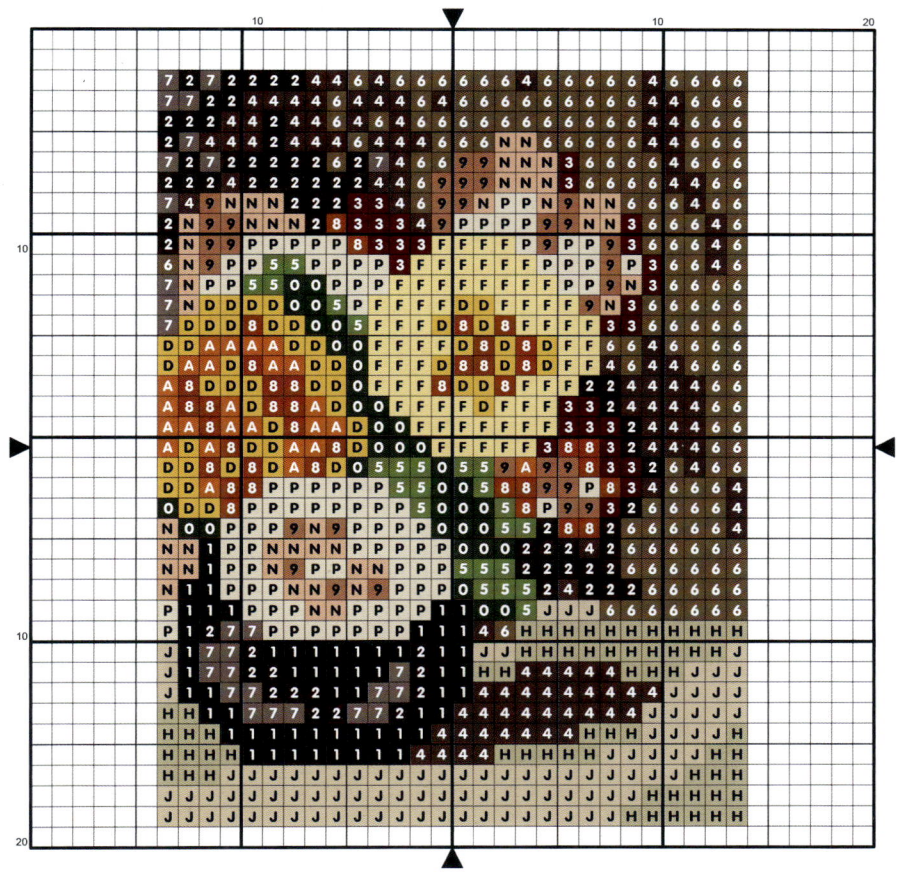

Symbol	Number	Color Name	Symbol	Number	Color Name
O	520	Wild Wood	1	3371	Peppercorn
2	938	Clove	3	814	Vin Rouge
4	09	Pine Marten	5	3347	Asparagus
6	640	Grey Cobblestone	7	451	Little Gray
8	3826	Fox	9	407	Fawn
A	976	Nutmeg	D	3821	Metallic Mango
F	677	Metallic Sand	H	644	Hemp
J	3033	Ashes	N	950	Beige
P	3866	Garlic White			

Pierre-Auguste Renoir

Still Life with Roses

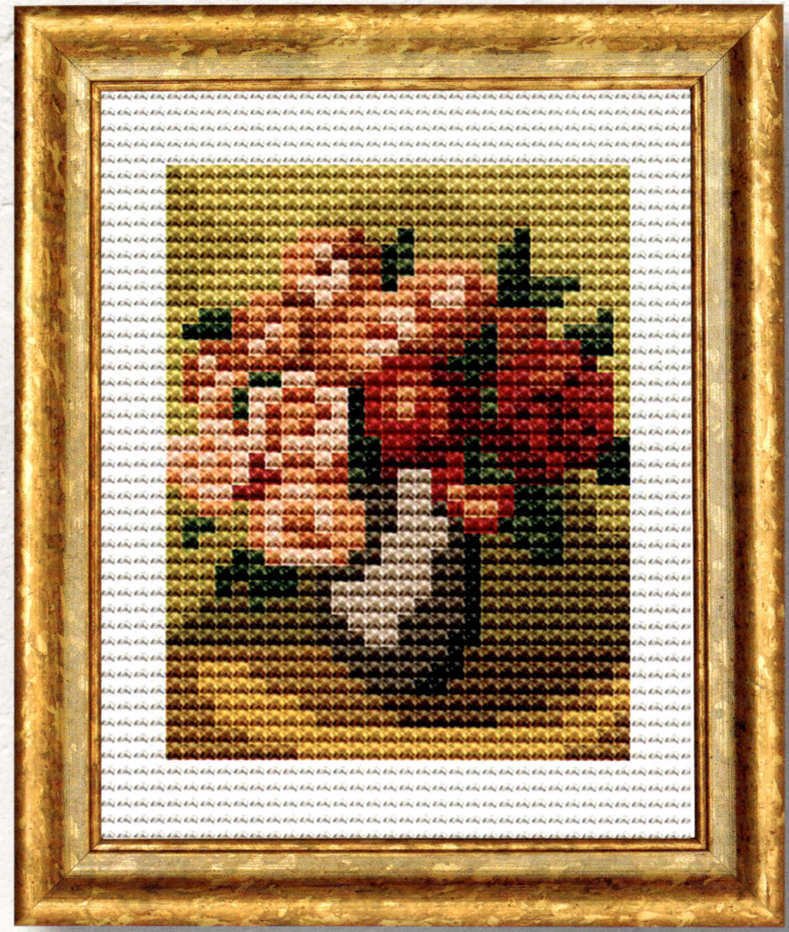

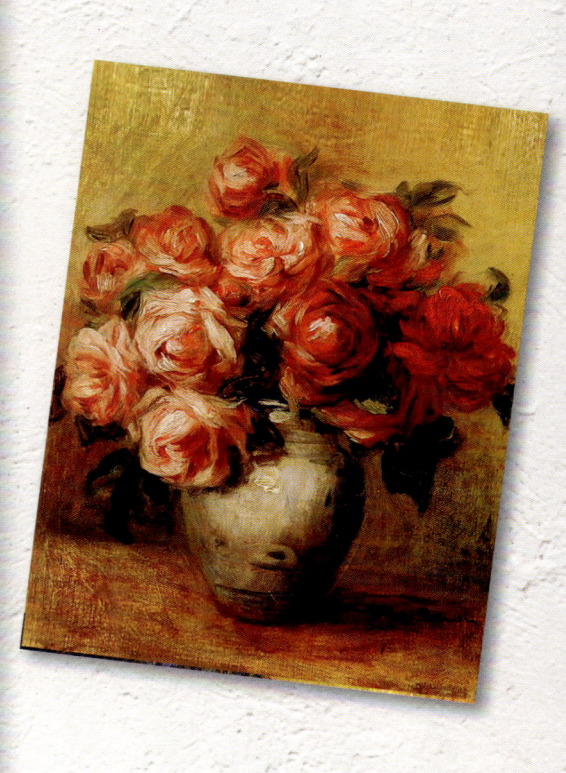

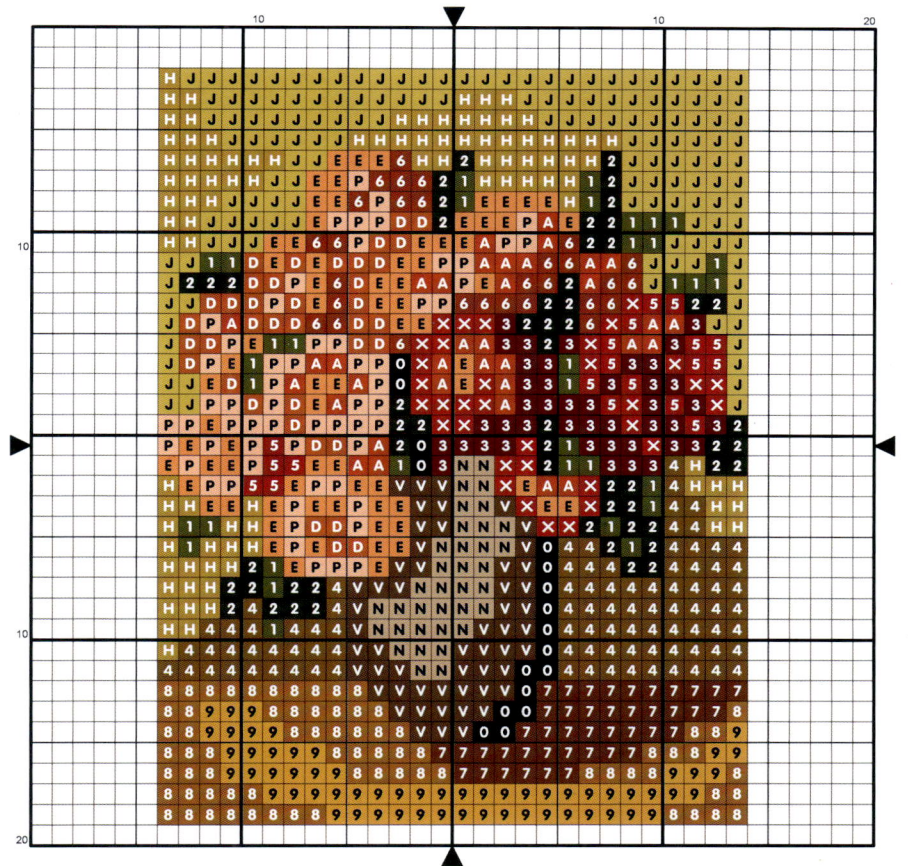

Symbol	Number	Color Name	Symbol	Number	Color Name
0	310	Metallic Black	1	3346	Artichoke
2	895	Bottle Green	3	815	Metallic Black Cherry
4	831	Bronze	5	347	Egyptian Red
6	301	Metallic Squirrel	7	869	Coffee
8	3829	Ochre Earth	9	3820	Sunshine
A	921	Tuscan Ochre	D	3776	Nut Brittle
E	402	Pottery	H	833	Brass
J	834	Dusty Sunflower	N	842	Beige Rope
P	754	Beige Rose	V	3790	Tree Bark
X	321	Metallic Carmine Red			

Henri Rousseau

Bouquet of Flowers with an Ivy Branch

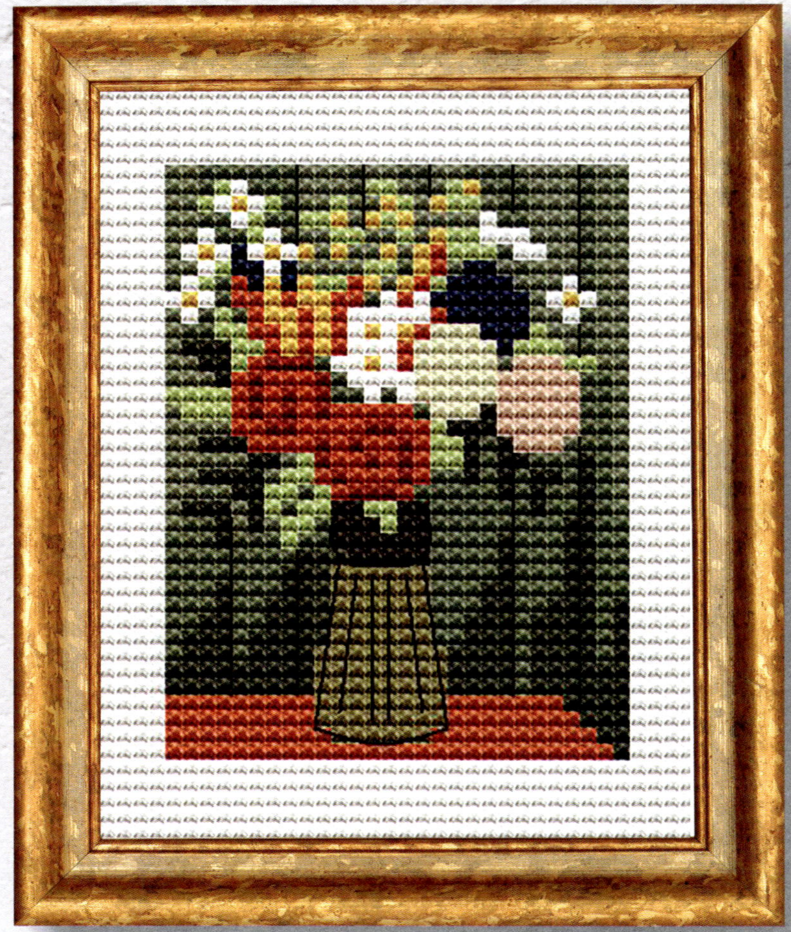

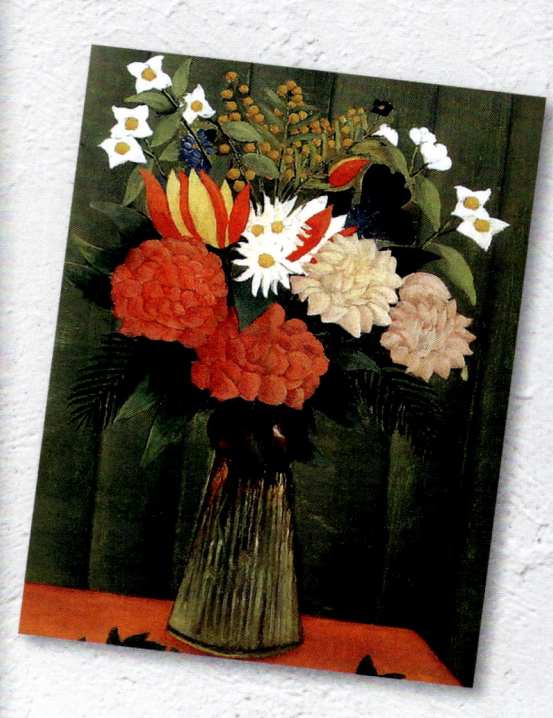

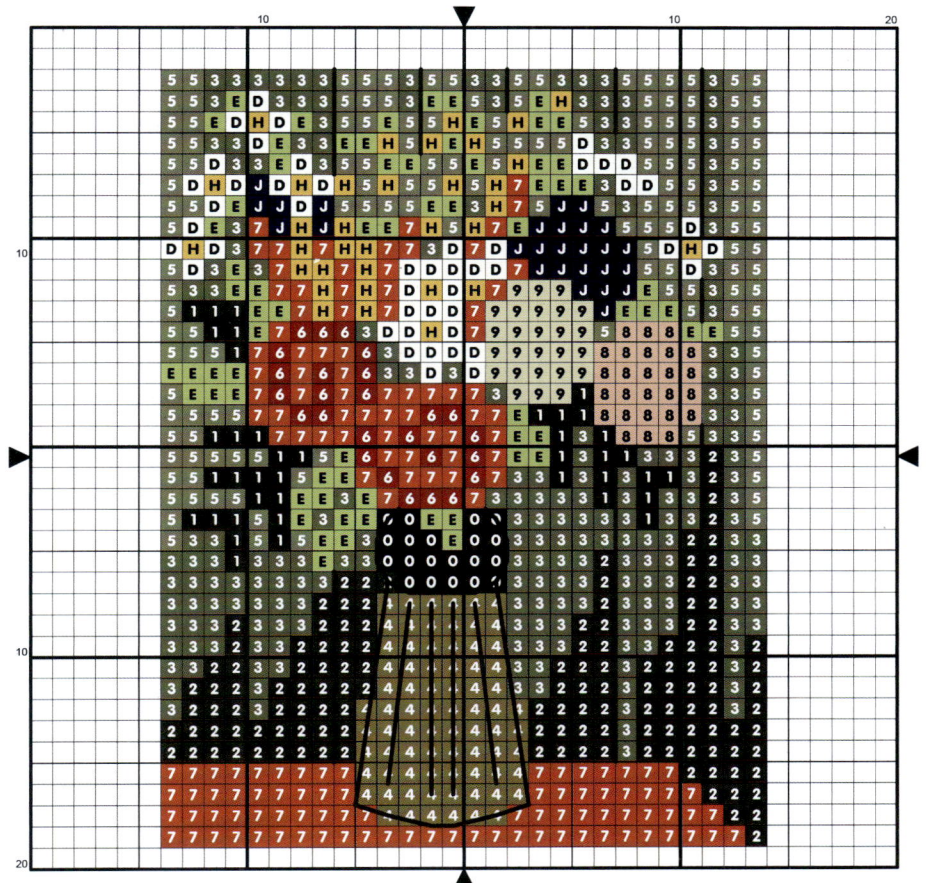

Symbol	Number	Color Name	Symbol	Number	Color Name
0	3371	Peppercorn	3	3363	Bullfrog
2	935	Undergrowth	5	522	Lattice Green
4	3012	Dried Moss	7	921	Tuscan Ochre
6	919	Terracotta Brown	9	10	Lemon Sherbert
8	950	Beige	E	3348	Scallion
D	3865	Edelweiss	J	336	Indigo Blue
H	3821	Metallic Mango	—	3371	Peppercorn
1	934	Seaweed	—	934	Seaweed

Henri Rousseau

Still Life

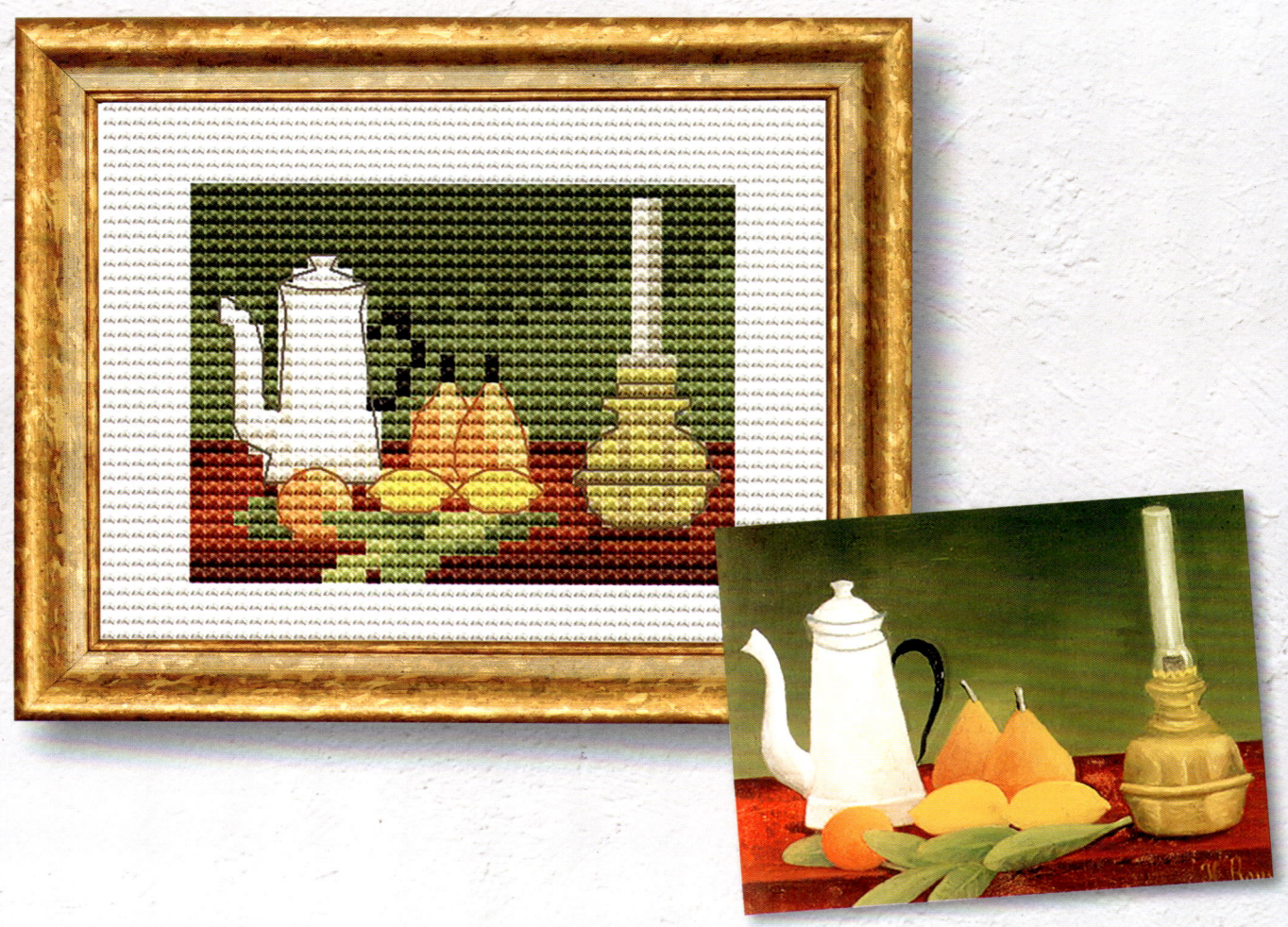

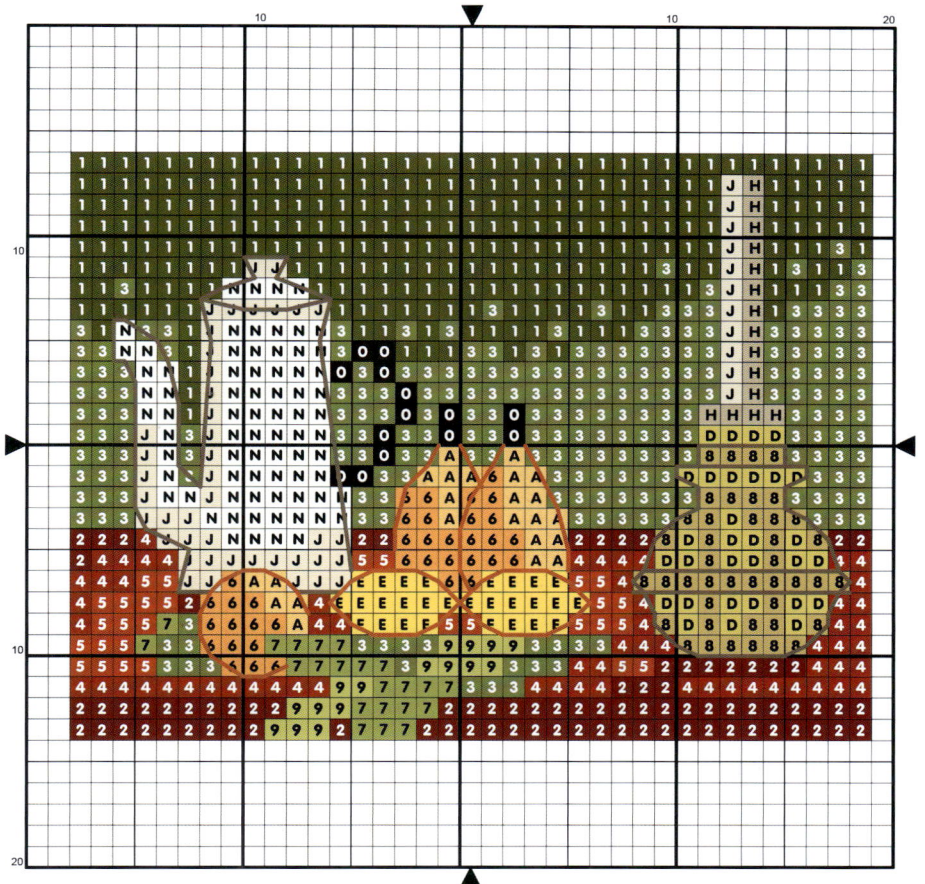

Symbol	Number	Color Name	Symbol	Number	Color Name
O	310	Metallic Black	3	3347	Asparagus
2	918	Rosewood	5	921	Tuscan Ochre
4	920	Sienna Ochre	7	471	Tarragon
6	3854	Chai Spice	9	472	Green Bud
8	3046	Biscuit	D	17	Maize
A	3855	Desert Winds	H	644	Hemp
E	726	Mimosa	N	3865	Edelweiss
J	ECRU	Ecru	—	646	Smoke Grey
1	3346	Artichoke	—	3776	Nut Brittle

H. Lyman Saÿen

Anemones

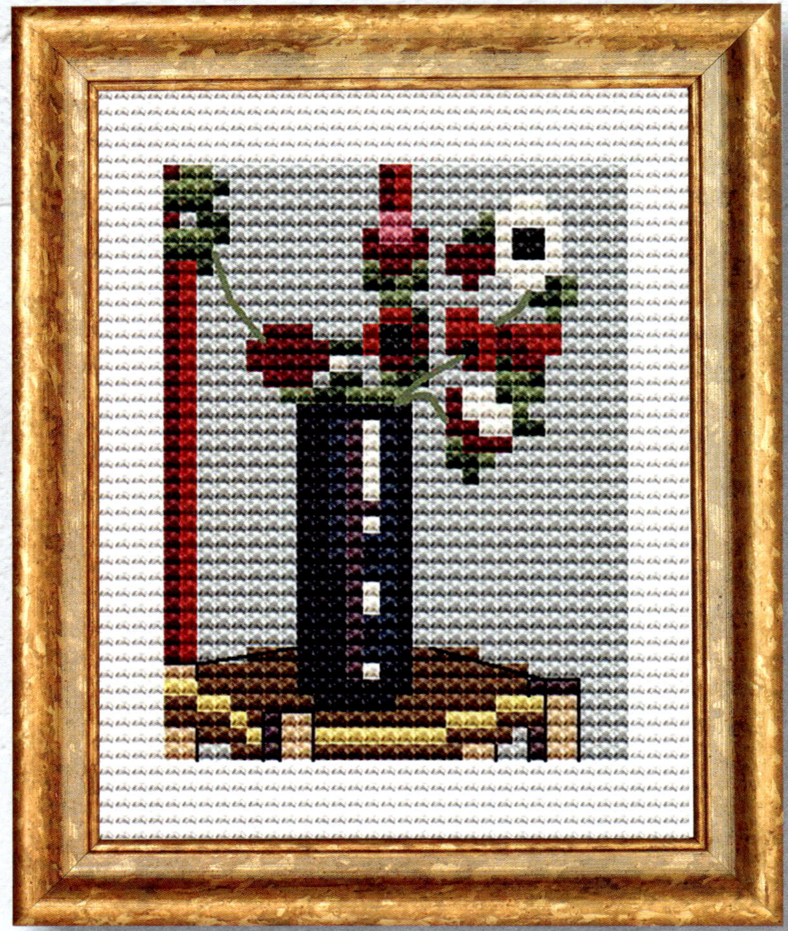

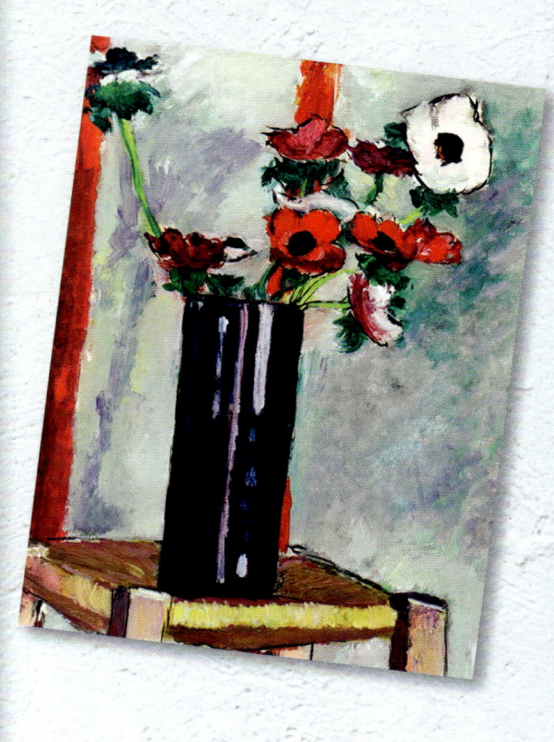

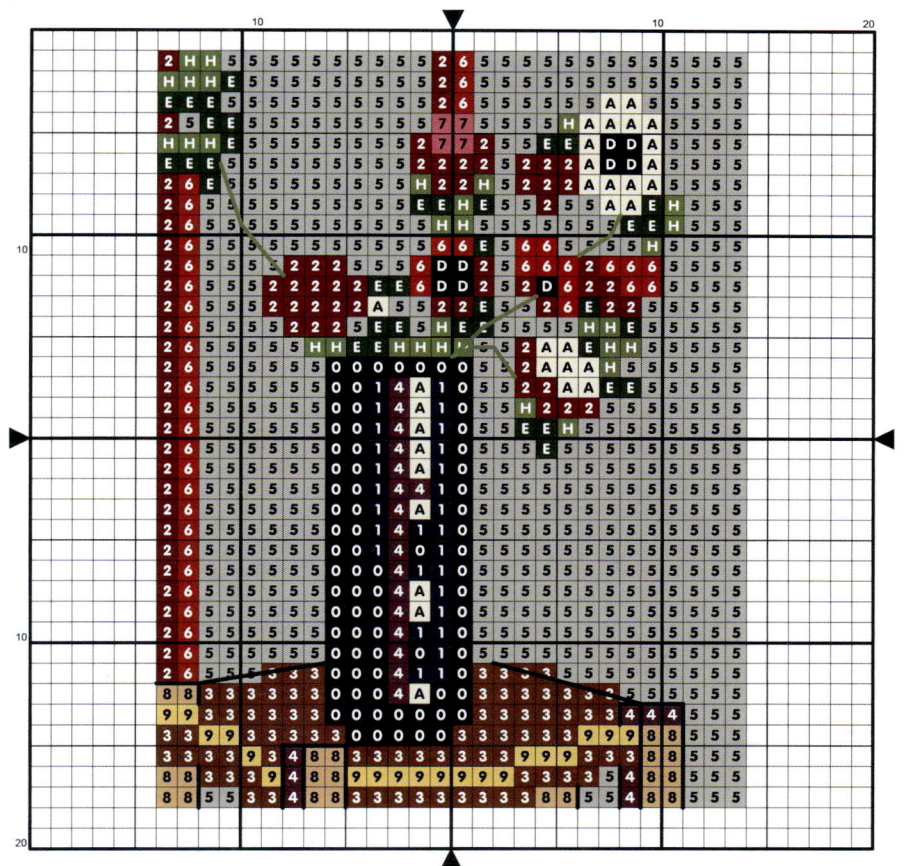

Symbol	Number	Color Name	Symbol	Number	Color Name
0	939	Elderberry Blue	3	869	Coffee
2	815	Metallic Black Cherry	5	928	Oyster Shell
4	3740	Gun Metal	7	3688	Pink Lupine
6	817	Japanese Red	9	3822	Corn Husk
8	738	Sahara	D	310	Metallic Black
A	712	Cream	H	3347	Asparagus
E	3345	Spinach	▬	310	Metallic Black
1	3750	Dark Petrol Blue	▬	3347	Asparagus

Robert John Thornton

Temple of Flora

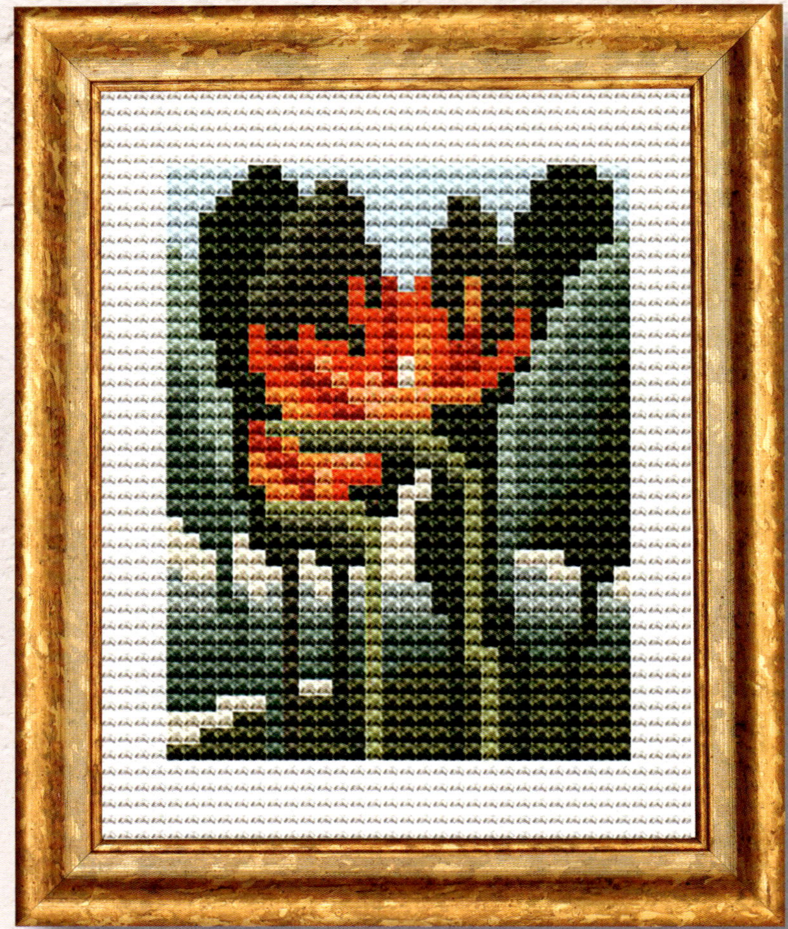

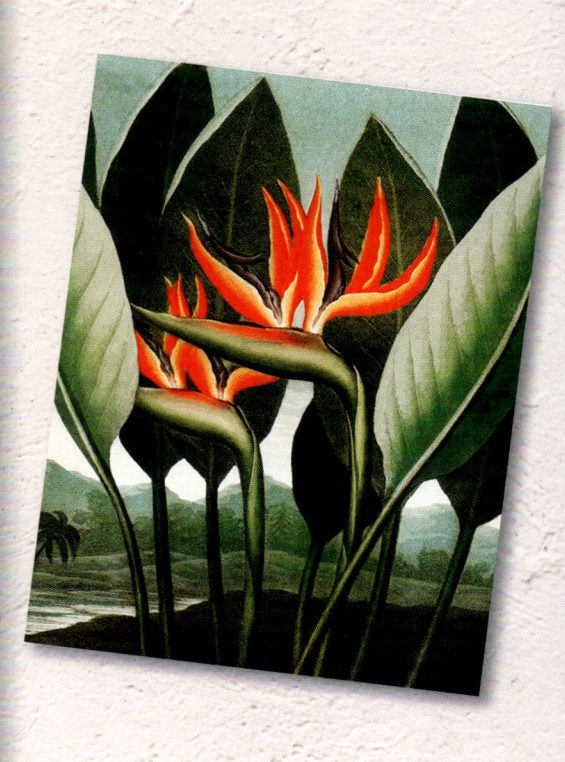

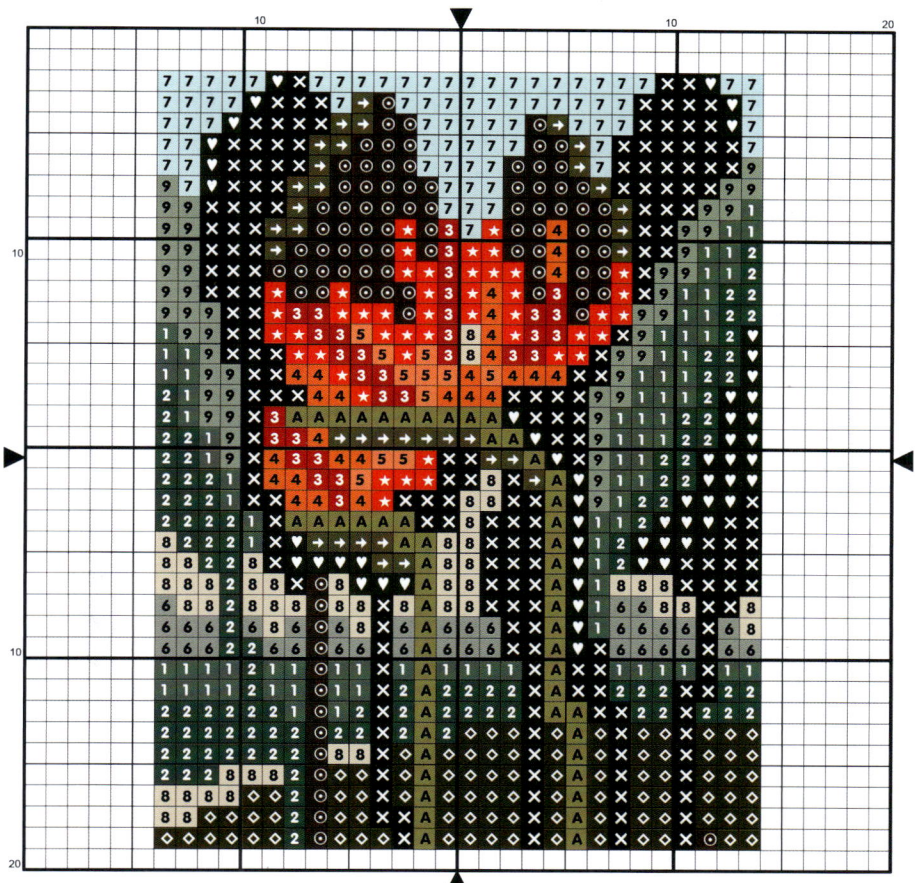

Symbol	Number	Color Name	Symbol	Number	Color Name
✖	895	Bottle Green	◉	3362	Conifer
◆	937	Moss	♥	3345	Spinach
➔	3363	Bullfrog	★	947	Sunset
1	3816	Serpent	2	3815	Almond Green
3	900	Blood Orange	4	741	Mandarin
5	3825	Muted Apricot	6	3813	Lichen Green
7	747	Pearlescent Blue Sea Mist	8	822	Cotton
9	3817	Poplar	A	3364	Sage

Floris Verster

Still Life with Zinnias in a Green Jar

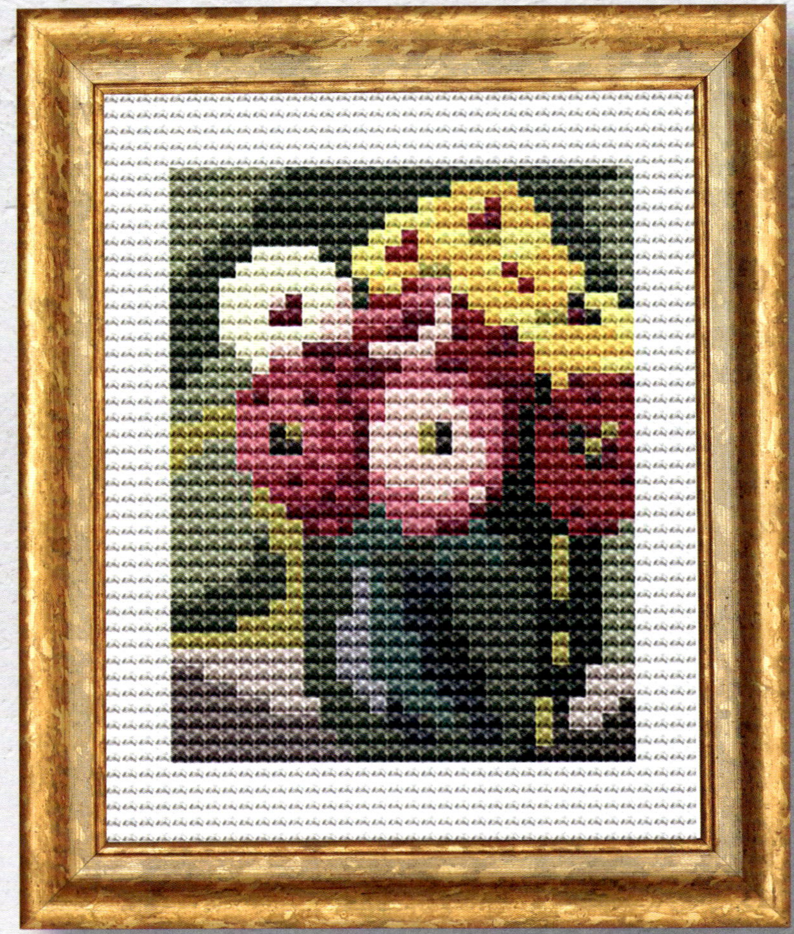

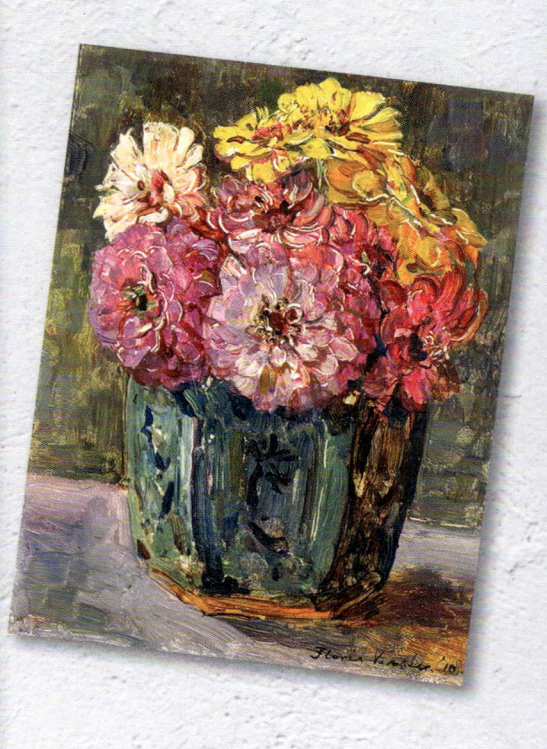

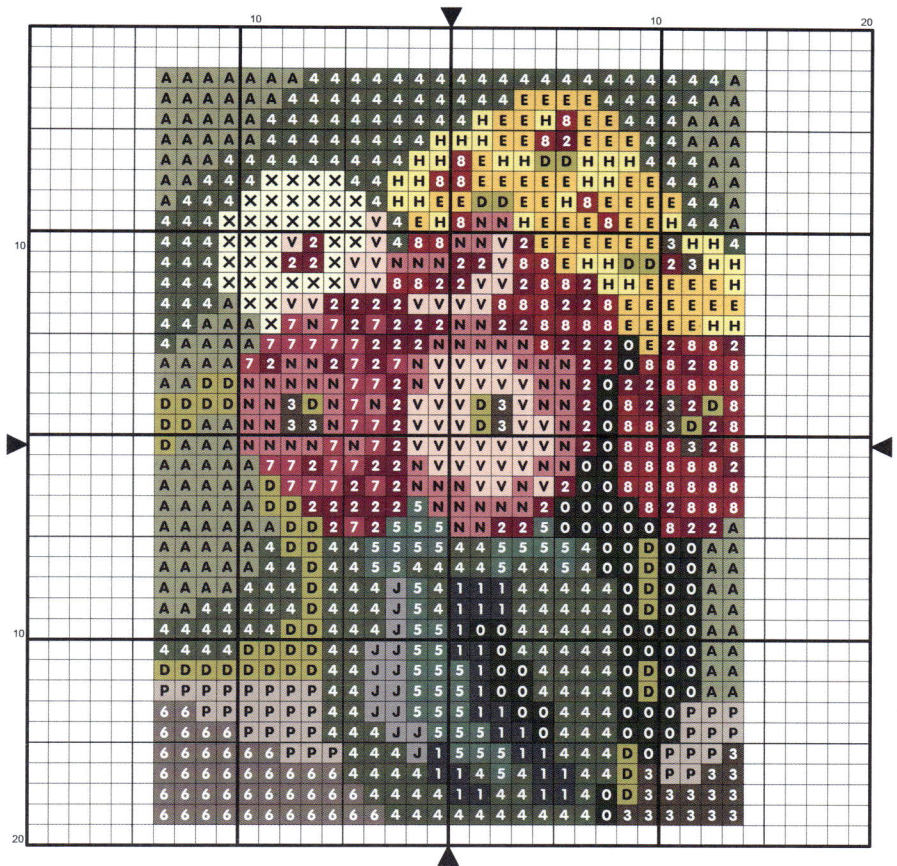

Symbol	Number	Color Name	Symbol	Number	Color Name
O	934	Seaweed	1	413	Iron
2	3803	Bordeaux	3	3787	Grey Wolf
4	645	Reindeer Grey	5	502	Almond Leaf
6	451	Little Gray	7	3687	Berry Smoothie
8	3350	Dragonfruit	A	523	Green Ash
D	734	Broken Olive	E	725	Buttercup
H	727	Primrose	J	03	Dust
N	3688	Pink Lupine	P	453	Dove Gray
V	225	Cherry Blossom	X	746	Pearlescent Vanilla

Black-and-White Charts

Pierre Bonnard
The Poppies

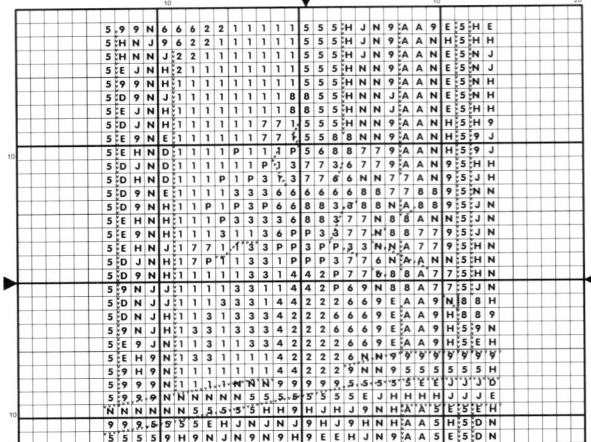

Paul Cézanne
Apples and Oranges

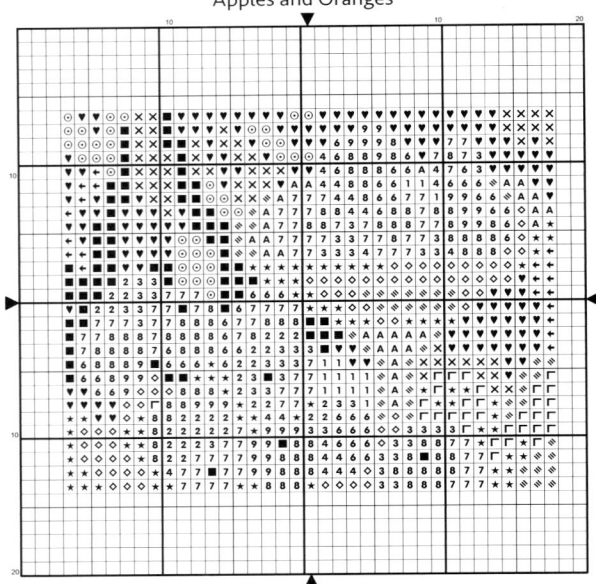

Gustave Caillebotte
Garden Rose and Blue Forget Me Nots in a Vase

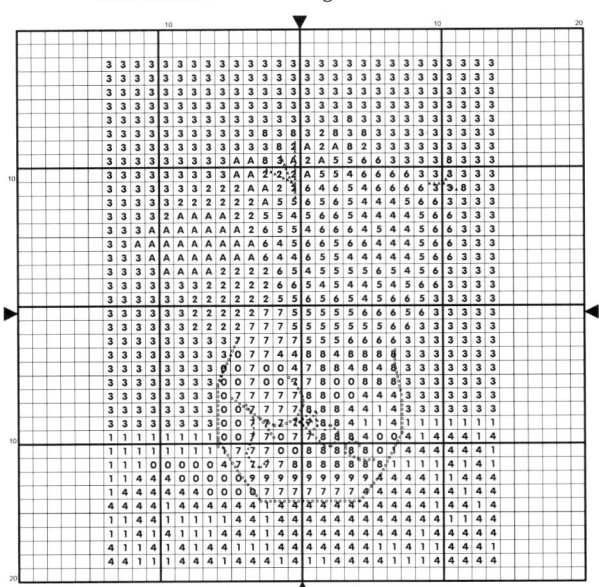

Paul Cézanne
Curtain, Jug and Fruit Bowl

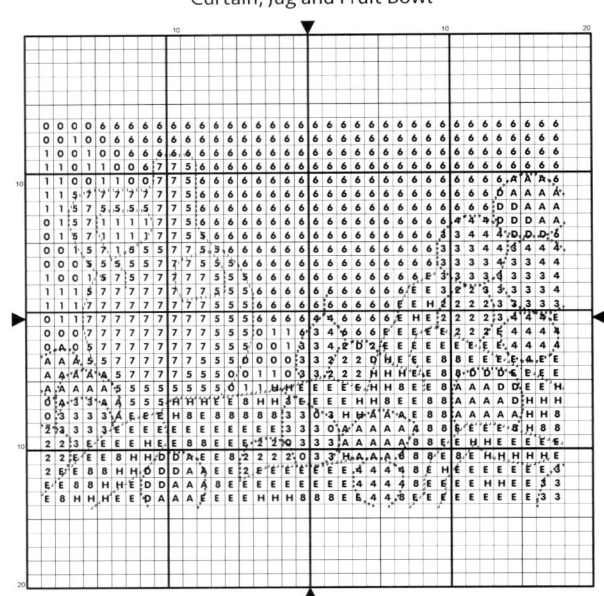

Paul Cézanne
Still Life with Apples

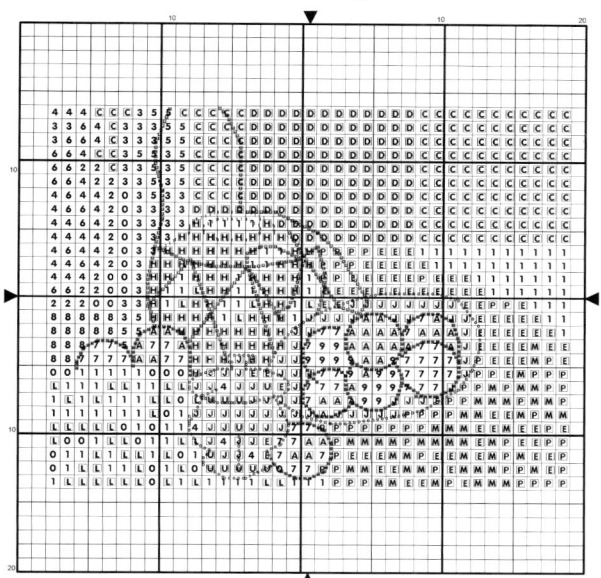

Paul Cézanne
Still Life with Skull

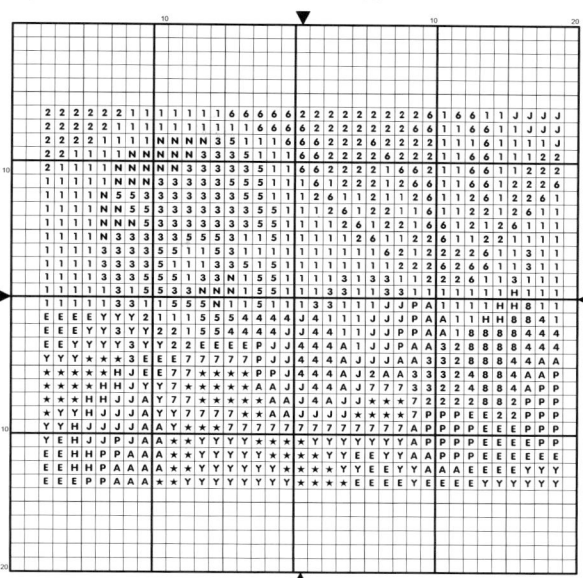

Paul Cézanne
Still Life with Apples and a Pot of Primroses

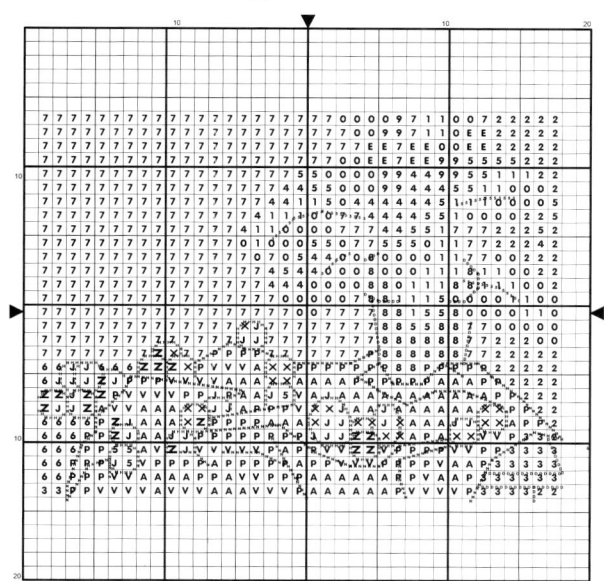

Paul Gauguin
Still Life with Oranges

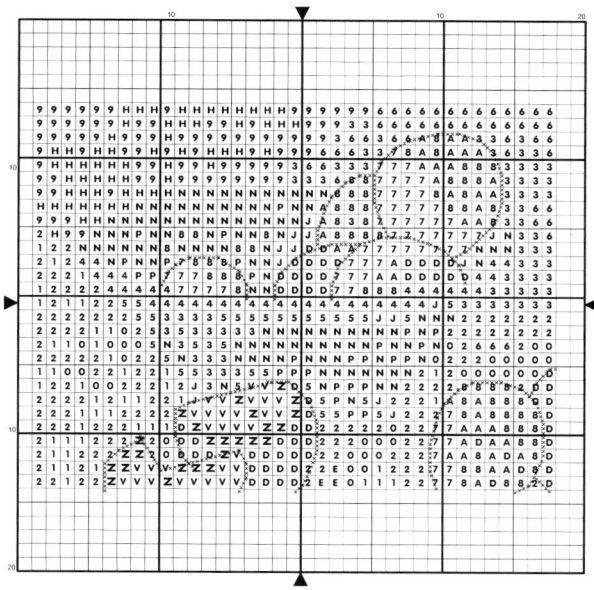

Paul Gauguin
Still Life with Teapot and Fruit

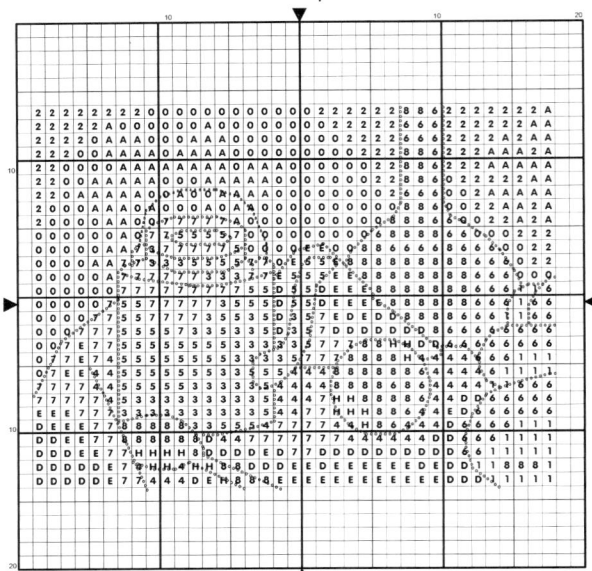

Vincent van Gogh
Majolica Jug with Wildflowers

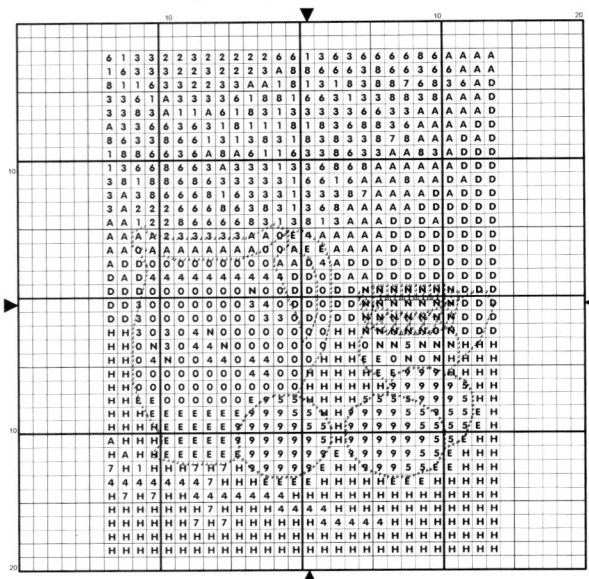

Vincent van Gogh
Irises

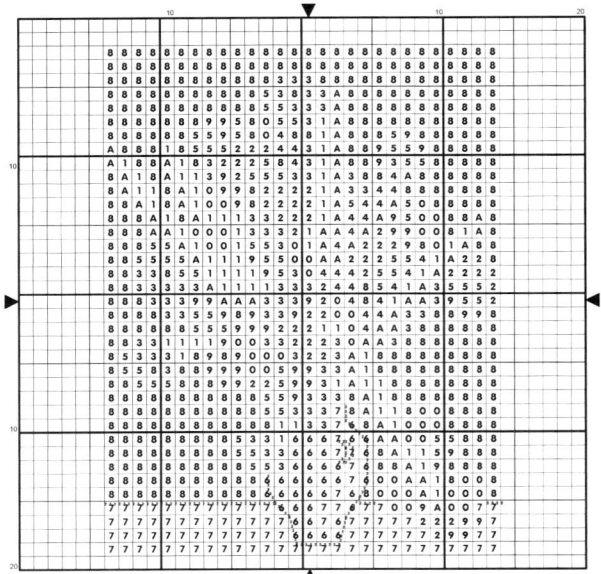

Vincent van Gogh
Sunflowers

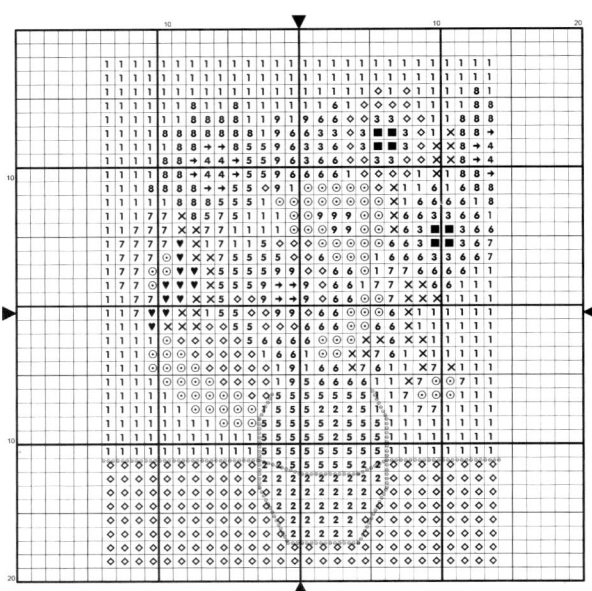

Vincent van Gogh
Three Sunflowers

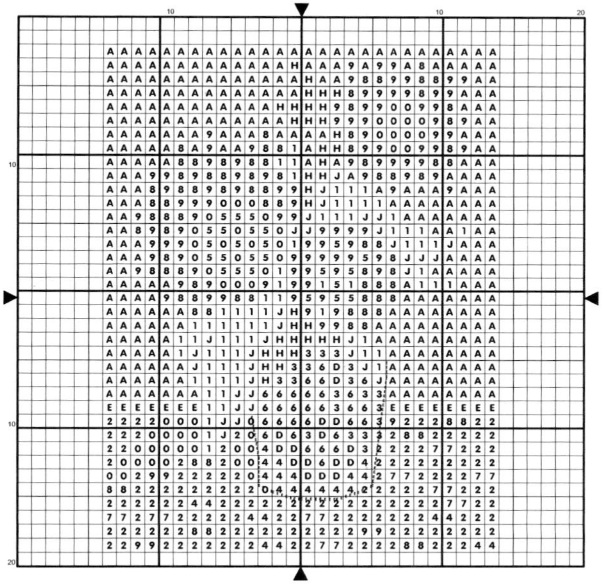

Vincent van Gogh
Vase with Carnations

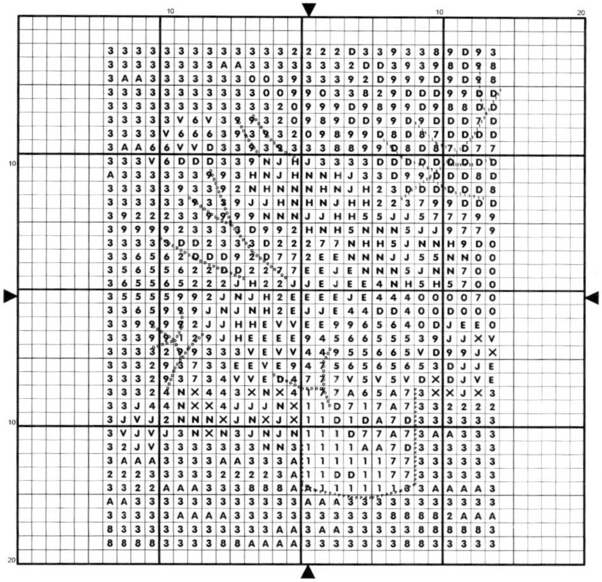

Vincent van Gogh
Vase of Roses

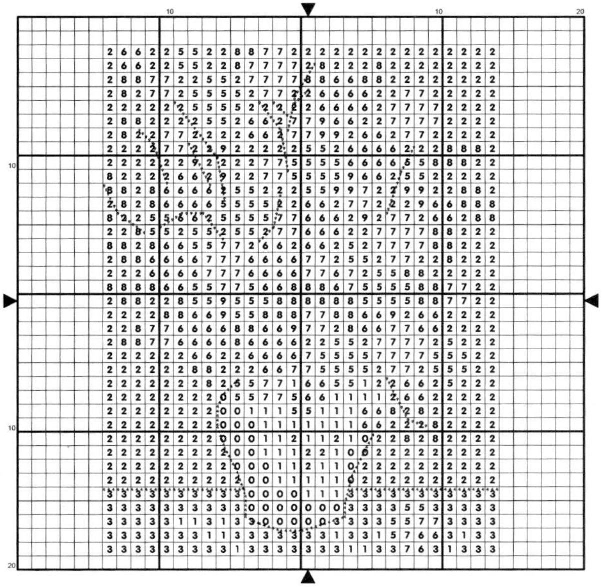

Vincent van Gogh
Vase with Oleanders and Books

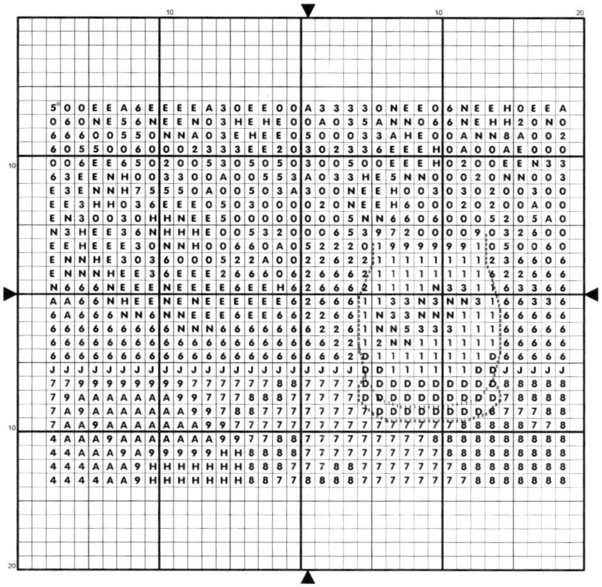

Vincent van Gogh
Vase with Poppies

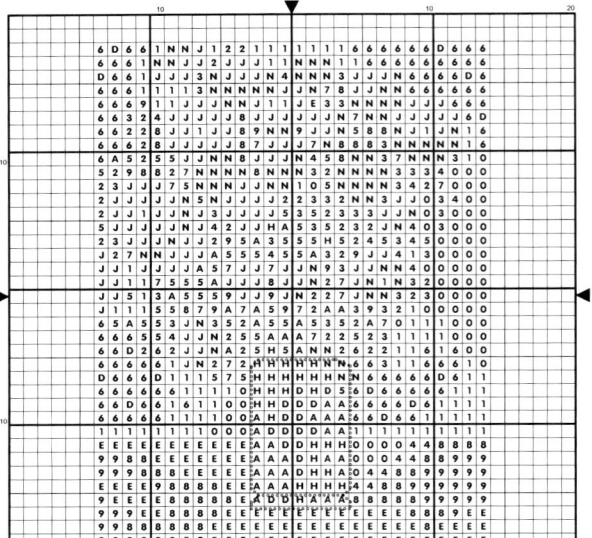

Shirley Hibberd
Various Ivy Leaves

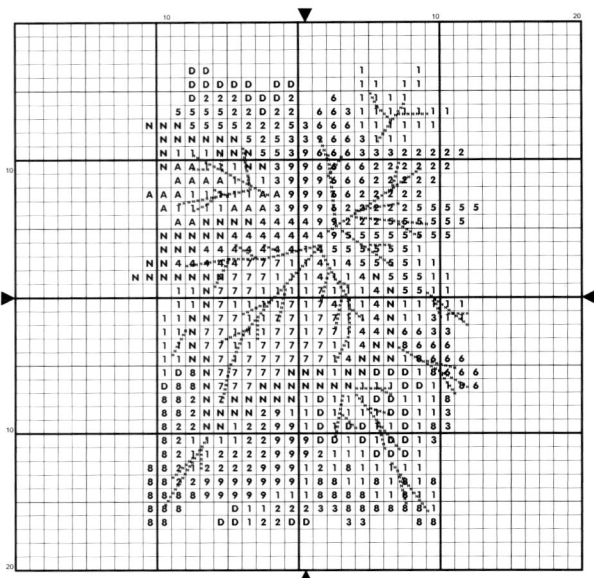

William Harnett
The Old Violin

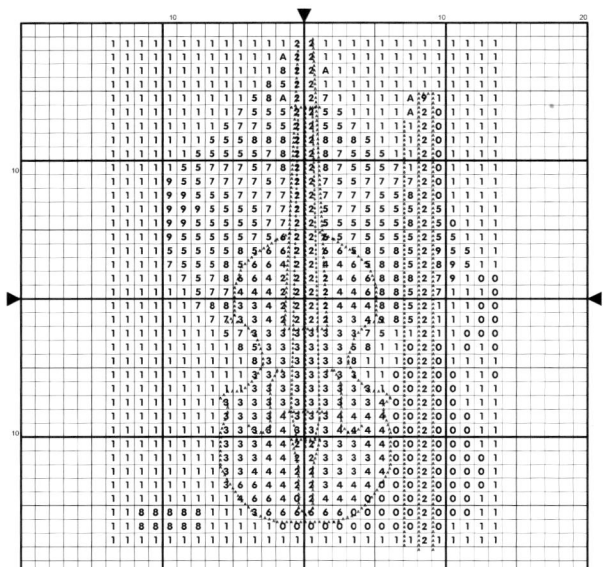

Nora Heysen
Spring Flowers

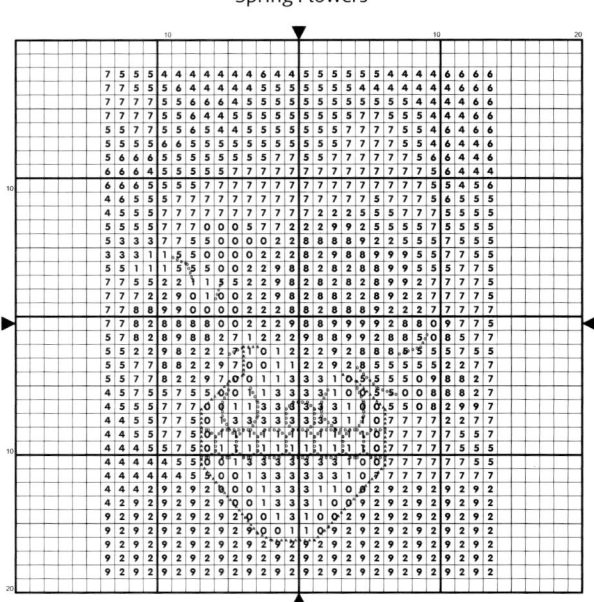

Michiel van Huysum
Branch with a Sunflower

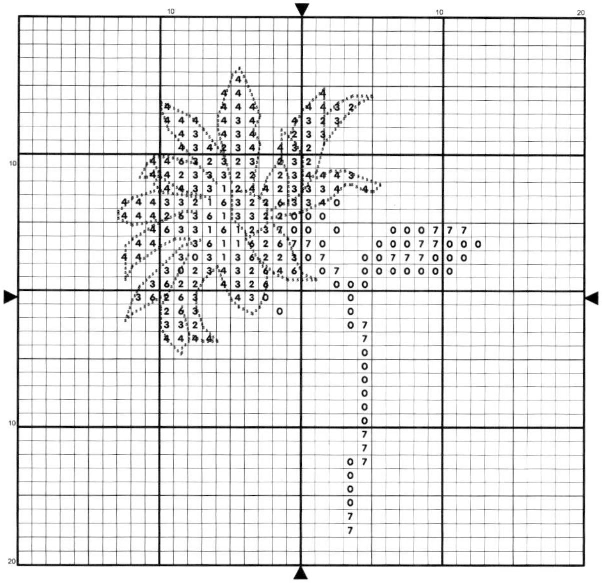

August Macke
The Ghost in the House Stalls–Still Life with a Cat

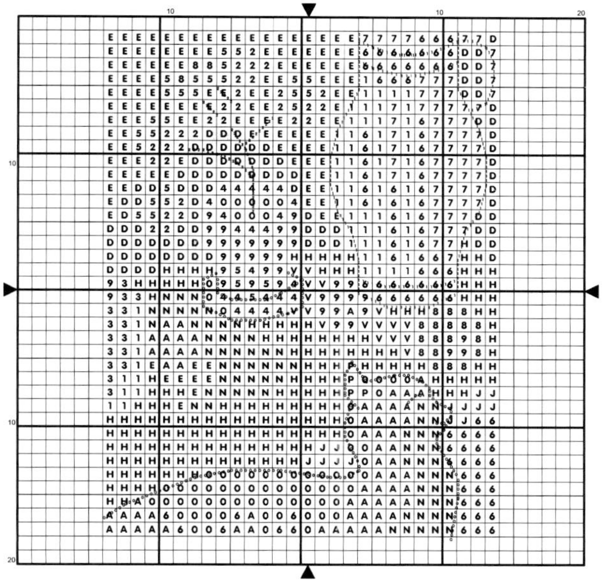

Jan van Kessel
Vanitas Still Life

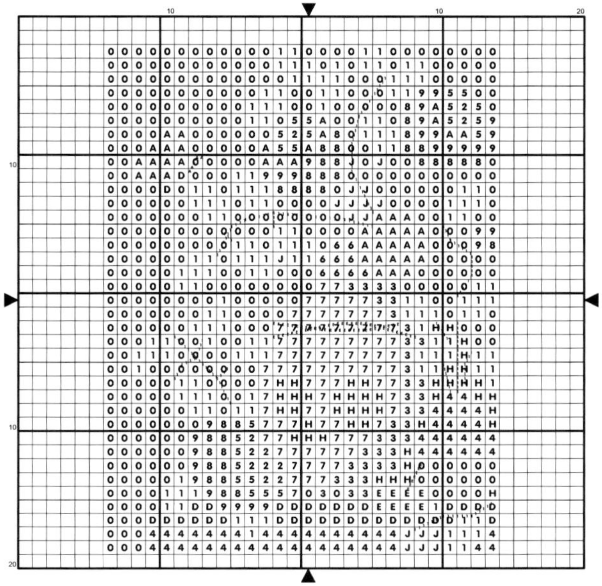

August Macke
Little Walter's Toys

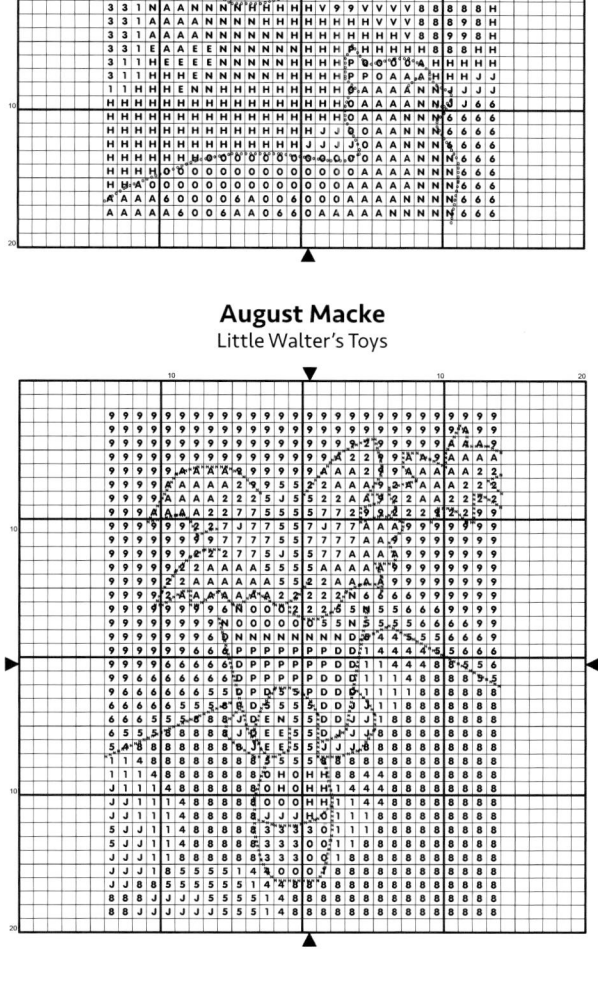

Édouard Manet
Moss Roses in a Vase

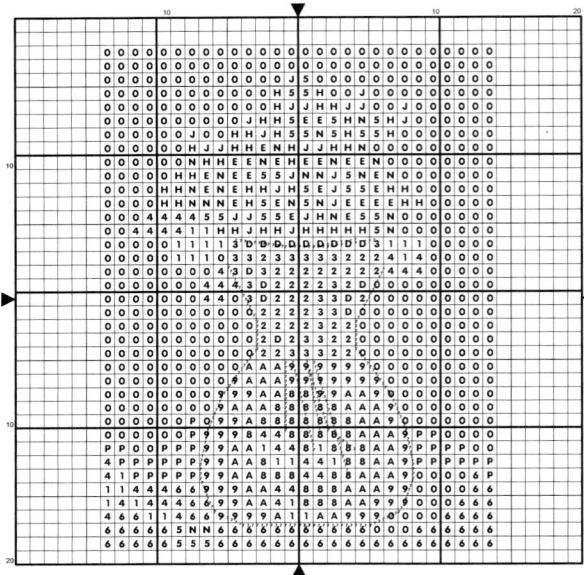

Henri Matisse
Geranium

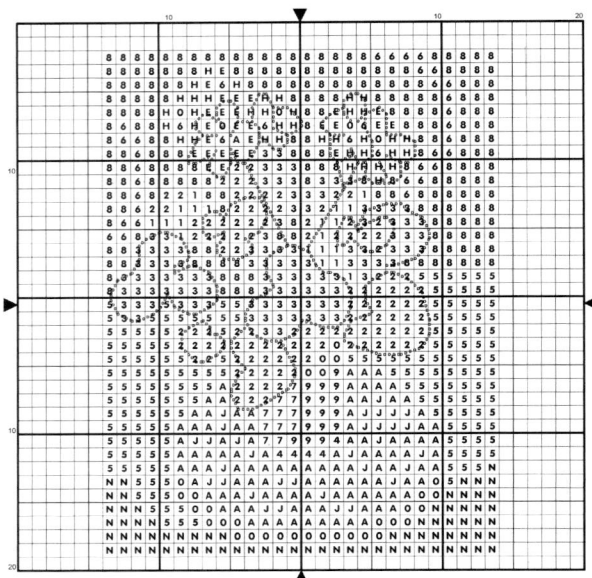

Henri Matisse
Daisies

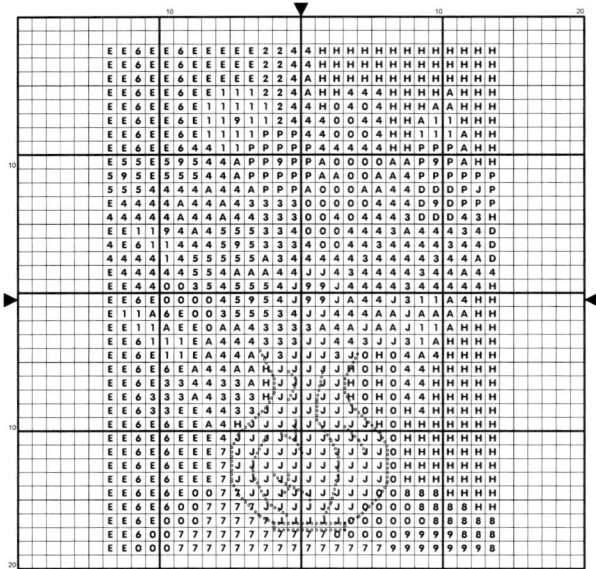

Henri Matisse
Vase of Flowers in Front of the Window

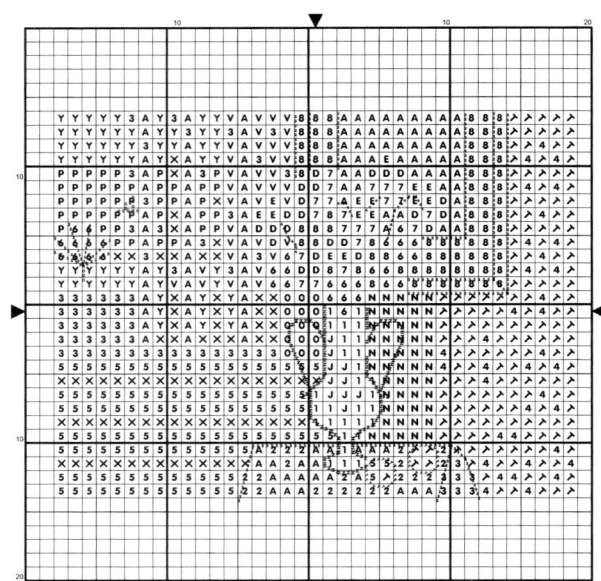

Luis Egidio Meléndez
Still Life with Watermelons and Apples

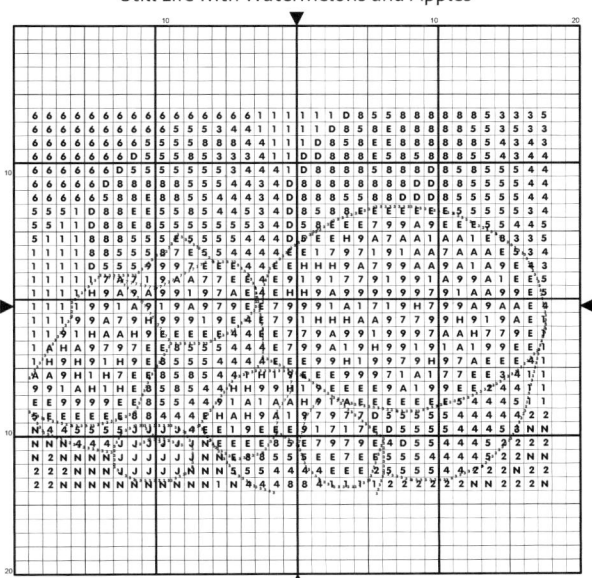

Claude Monet
Christmas Roses

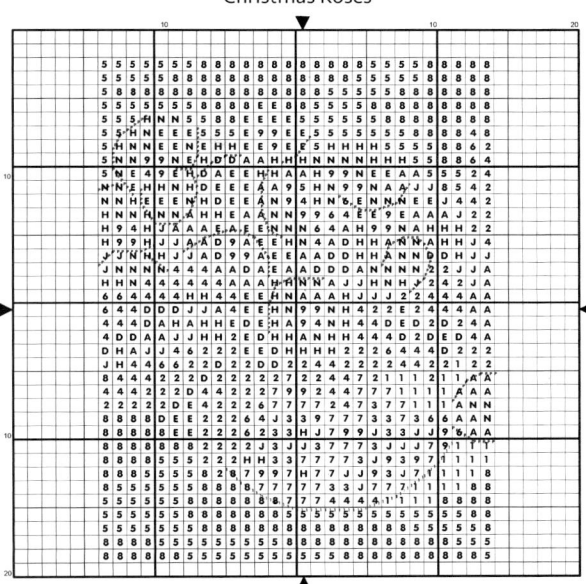

Claude Monet
Bouquet of Sunflowers

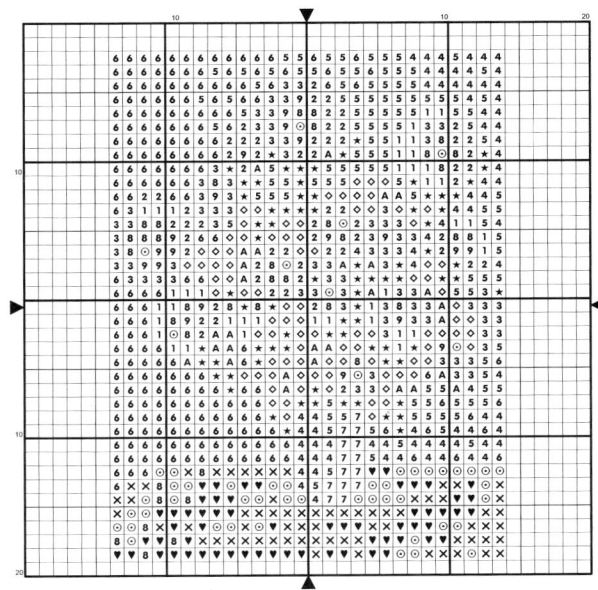

Claude Monet
Chrysanthemums

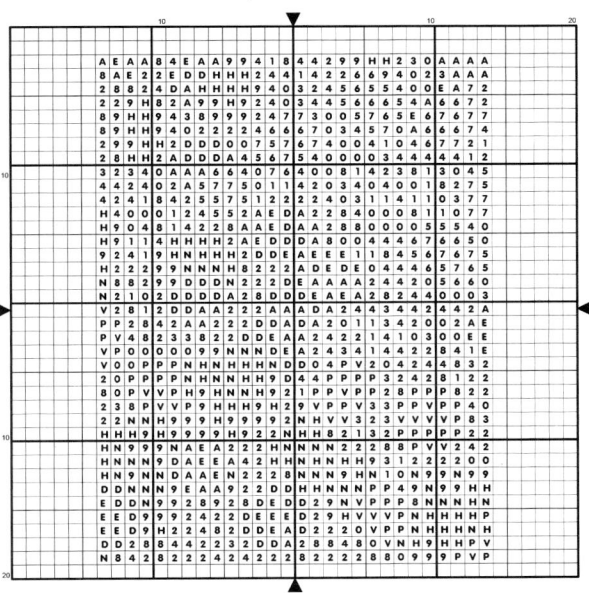

Claude Monet
Nasturtiums in a Blue Vase

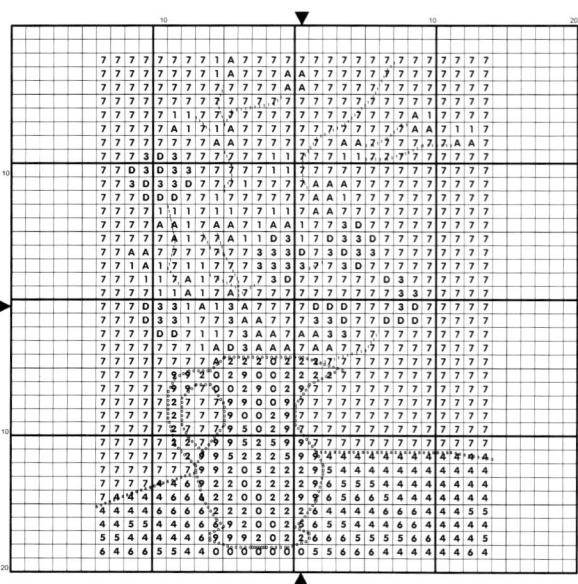

Claude Monet
Water Lilies

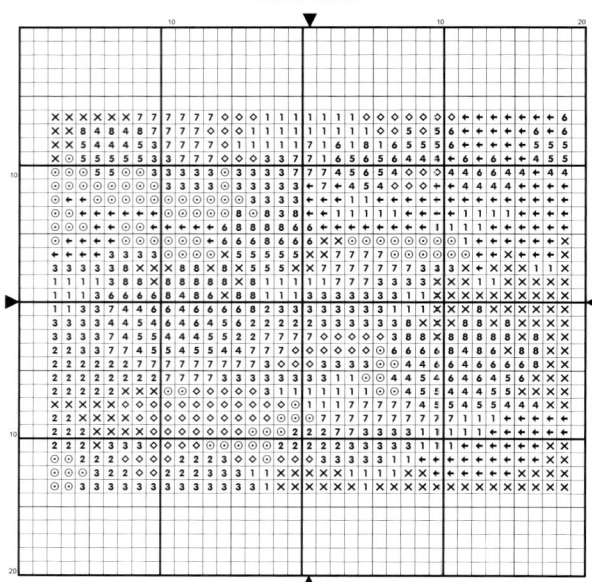

Claude Monet
Three Pots of Tulips

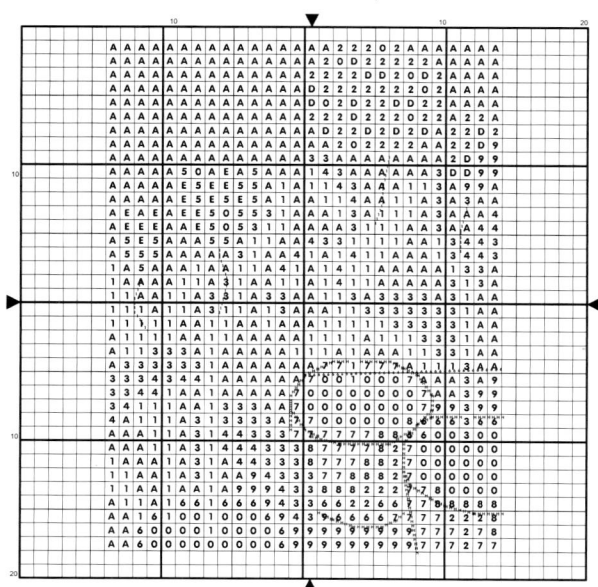

Odilon Redon
Poppies and Daisies

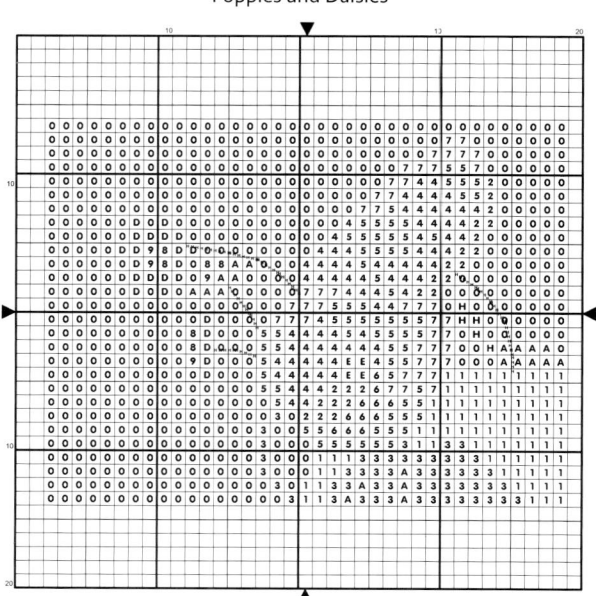

Pierre-Joseph Redouté
Vase of Flowers

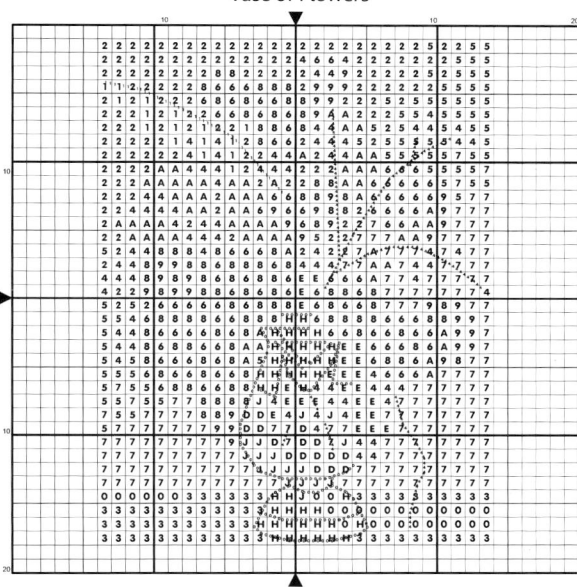

Pierre-Auguste Renoir
Bouquet of Roses

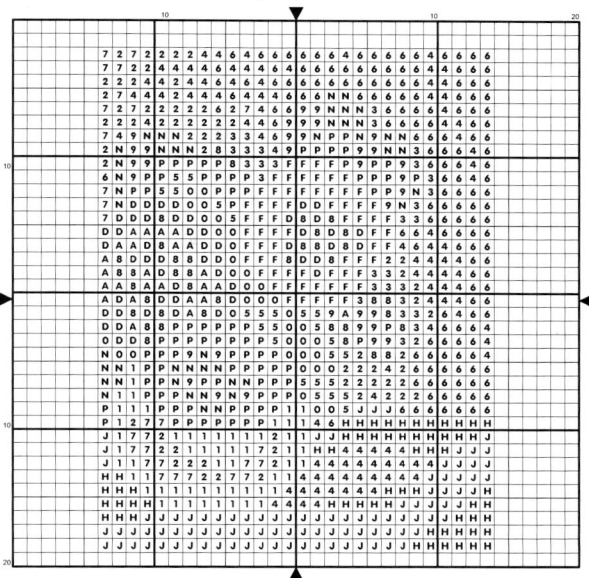

Pierre-Auguste Renoir
Anemones

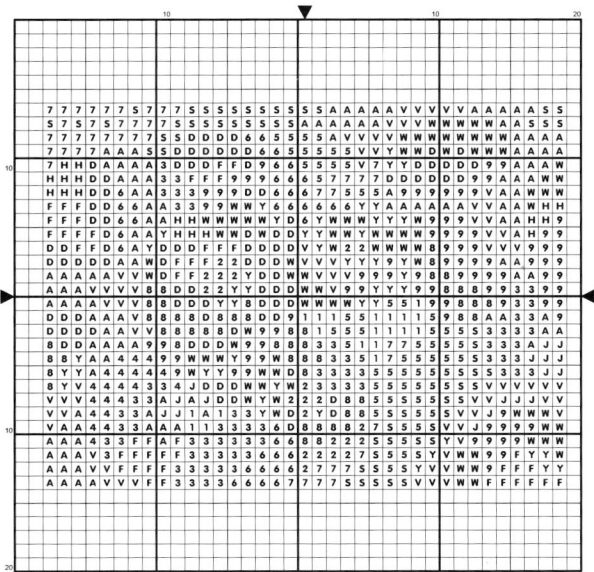

Pierre-Auguste Renoir
Still Life with Roses

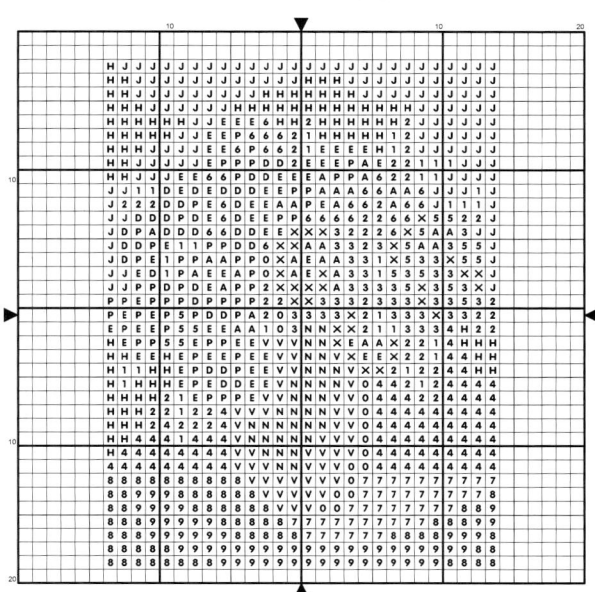

Henri Rousseau
Bouquet of Flowers with an Ivy Branch

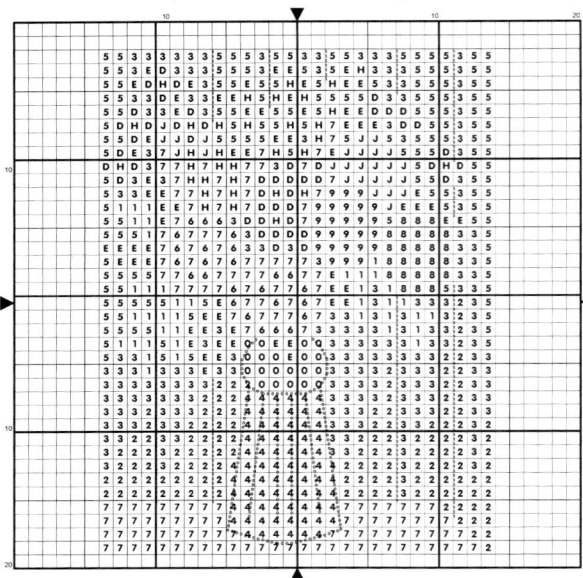

H. Lyman Saÿen
Anemones

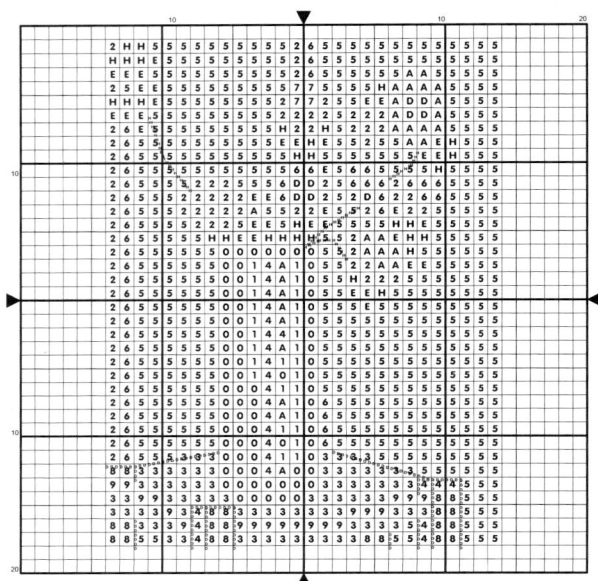

Henri Rousseau
Still Life

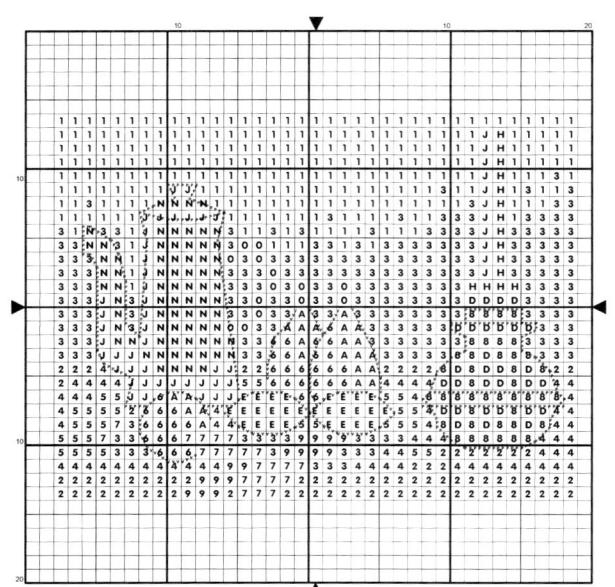

Robert John Thornton
Temple of Flora

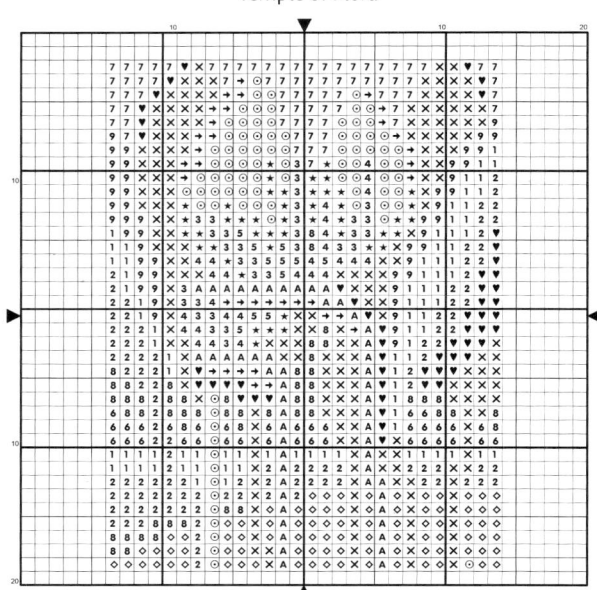

Floris Verster
Still Life with Zinnias in a Green Jar

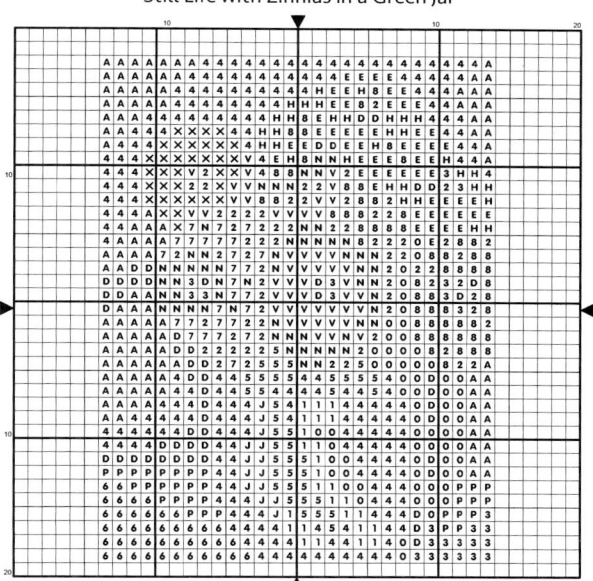

About Us

Ale Pico

Graphic designer, mum of two. I truly enjoyed the process of selection and adaptation of the mini masterpieces in this book, so I hope you enjoy stitching them too! I live in Spain with my two kids, husband, and dog.

Gaby Pico

Architect, mum of two. I have designed all the patterns, trying to make each of them as similar as possible to the originals. I love the fine details of making each little *X*! I live in Mexico with my two kids, husband, dog, and little pets.